The Last Essene

By

Wayne-Daniel Berard

With

Dr. Sylvia Hammerman

THE LAST ESSENE
Copyright © 2024 Wayne-Daniel Berard
All Rights Reserved.
Published by Unsolicited Press.
Printed in the United States of America.
First Edition.

No part of this book may be used or reproduced in any manner whatsoever without written permission except in the case of brief quotations embodied in critical articles or reviews. People, places, and notions in these poems are from the author's imagination; any resemblance to real persons or events is purely coincidental.

Attention schools and businesses: for discounted copies on large orders, please contact the publisher directly.

For information contact:
Unsolicited Press
Portland, Oregon
www.unsolicitedpress.com
orders@unsolicitedpress.com
619-354-8005

Cover Designer: Kathryn Gerhardt
Artwork by: Greta Kessler
Artwork Optimizer: **Rob Schadt**
Editor: Kristen Marckmann

ISBN: 978-1-963115-17-8

OTHER BOOKS BY WAYNE-DANIEL BERARD

The Realm of Blessing

The Man Who Remembered Heaven: Stories from the Center

How Air Is

Lost Final Chapter of Hermann Hesse's Siddhartha

The Last Essene

PRELUDE

Stained Glass

Once there was a traveler on a long journey. The road passed through a village that appeared to have seen better days. The village square was unkempt; long tufts of grass pushed between its bricks, while in its fountain, unmoved water merely stood in pools of green inertia. But at one end of the square did stand a rather magnificent cathedral.

The traveler was glad, for this cathedral was famous, world renowned for its exquisite and powerful stained glass. Indeed, the route had been chosen in hope of encountering just this sight.

Not knowing the local customs, the traveler looked about. The square was empty, but approaching from its opposite corner came a laborer, pushing a heavy cart.

The traveler called out, "Good day to you, friend. Can you tell me, at what hours is the cathedral open?"

"Open?" replied the laborer, resting the cart upon the dusty bricks. "Why would y' want to know that?"

"I've traveled far," came the reply, "and have farther still to go. But I would dearly love to look upon the stained glass, about which I've heard so much."

"Yer lookin' at it," answered the laborer with a motion toward the cathedral.

The traveler looked across the square. The tall windows were, of course, visible. But from the outside, they were the color of very wet mud.

"Oh no," said the traveler. "I want to see the stained glass from the *inside*. Is this possible?"

"From the inside?" puzzled the laborer. "Why bother? Y' can see right from here, there's nothin' special to see."

The traveler felt confused.

"Is this your home?"

The laborer nodded.

"Then surely you know what I'm talking about? How different it is on the inside?"

"Never been inside," answered the laborer, picking up the cart handles. "Too busy. Work to do."

As the laborer moved away, the traveler called after him. "But are the doors open? Is it alright to go inside?"

"Suit yourself," said the laborer over one shoulder.

The traveler approached the cathedral. Its great doors were indeed unlocked, though their hinges creaked and crackled with rust. But the light inside! What is to be said? It was as far from mud as full-throated song from thin sheets of music, as the soft curve of Eve's neck from the grizzle of an old rib. The traveler remained a long while, a very long while, deciding when to move on. If ever.

And during that time, the great doors made nary a sound. The traveler was entirely alone. "Is this my choice?" the question grew within. "Light? Or companionship?"

CHAPTER 1

The Roads All Taken

The scene shifted. I was waiting outside the compound gate for La'nah and her family. We were going to walk together to Friday night services. Eventually, she, her mother, and the servant (whose name I now knew was "Cush") came along. We walked deeper into the Jewish Quarter, the servant and I in the front and La'nah and her mother behind. We came to a smallish building with a white dome; the building looked a bit worse for wear. We walked through an outer room; when I turned around, I could see a wooden cabinet with closed doors beside the entrance of the synagogue. We walked into the main room; it had a dirt floor with an aisle kept open down the center. Some people sat on wooden benches, some on the floor. There were men, women and children. We sat on the right side (as we entered), Cush, La'nah, her mother, and me all in a row on two benches. I was surprised that the servant sat with us. Up ahead was a bima (reader's/speaker's station) and behind and beside it, more benches. Against the far wall was another cabinet with closed doors.

The scene described is an event from about CE 90–100, in Alexandria, Egypt. The person remembering it is me, Wayne-

Daniel Berard, English and Humanities professor, interfaith clergy-person, and newly appointed Director of Spiritual Life and Chaplain of the college in which I taught. But the person experiencing the event is likewise me—or the me I once had been—Yosiah, called Yossi, an orphan taken in by the Essenes (ancient Jewish mystics and ascetics), a survivor of war's decimation, a Torah scholar, student of Wisdom Traditions of many sorts, and teacher.

I am sitting in the seventh of what would be twelve session of past-life regression led by Dr. Sylvia Hammerman.

A few months previous, I'd received a call in my office that both the Academic *and* Student Services Deans wished to see me. *What kind of trouble was I in?* I asked myself as I proceeded to their building. But when I arrived, both Deans seemed the opposite of ominous. Had I heard that the College Chaplain, a wonderful man and outstanding Catholic priest, had been reassigned to be a pastor? I had not, but it did not surprise me. A former Catholic seminarian myself (and former Catholic), I was very familiar with the priest shortage. Diocese all over the country were removing men from other positions and reassigning them to the parishes.

The Deans then informed me that our particular diocese was not going to assign another chaplain to us. "You're interfaith clergy, and we're a multi-faith community," one of them continued, we'd like to offer you the position of Director of Spiritual Life and Chaplain of the College. It's part-time; you'll receive a one-course release from your full-time teaching duties."

THE LAST ESSENE

I felt thrilled and entirely validated by the offer. I taught English, Philosophy, and Religious Studies at the College, and was generally seen by students, professors, and staff alike as "the spiritual guy" on the faculty. Many people from across the span of college life would come to my office to talk, be heard, seek counsel, or just to have who they were be entirely welcomed! My own background was very interfaith, indeed—an adoptee into a Catholic family, I'd always been quite spiritually oriented. I'd entered Franciscan seminary at fourteen, taken a leave of absence I didn't ask for at nineteen. My spiritual searching had brought me to stints in a number of communities and traditions, and I had been very heavily influenced by the East; I was a daily meditator and used meditation as a teaching and learning tool in my classes (thank God for tenure!). My involvement with the Peace Abbey, an interfaith center for peace and justice, had resulted in my commission as a Peace Chaplain, an interfaith clergy-person. Eventually, I entered into my adoption search, which brought me to the discovery that I was Jewish. This led me on yet another set of amazing spiritual adventures. Years of study of Torah as a Spiritual Path with the luminous Rabbi Alan Ullman, sharing depth, breadth, and height with seekers of all traditions and none, had ushered me here.

"You will be the spiritual leader of the community," one Dean said.

"But what do I do?" I asked.

"Exactly what you're doing now," the other responded. "Don't change a thing."

I replied that I never made any decision of import without speaking with The Lovely Christine, my wife and Great Love. But I think everyone in the room knew what the answer would be.

CHAPTER 2

The Variegated Life

We like to think of religions and spiritualities as a being all of a piece; Christianity is Christianity, Judaism is Judaism, etc. And that's it.

But in truth, all faith traditions and spiritualities are patchworks of irregular colors and streaks, differing beliefs and customs, layered one over the other, all showing through in their own ways, oftentimes without our even knowing it.

It is much the same with people. I was coming to find that the person I referred to as "me" had an equally streaked and varied make-up, and just not in in terms of forgotten or repressed childhood experiences or the impact of extended family patterns on the way I lived now. I was beginning to understand that, like the religions and philosophies I taught in my classes, I myself was an ongoing cumulation of many incarnations over time.

WAYNE-DANIEL BERARD

Faith was variegated. And so, apparently, was I.

One of the first decisions I made upon becoming Director of Spiritual Life and Chaplain was to listen—broadly and deeply. Although I'd been a faculty member of my college for twenty years, I did not want to simply assume that I knew what my community wanted or needed from its chaplain. So, with the help of the Psychology Department, I assembled a survey on exactly that, and shared it with students, faculty and staff (thankfully, ours is a small school). One of the most telling questions turned out to be this one:

"If you could have God right in front of you (however you understand the term) and could ask one question and get an answer, what would it be?"

My favorite response came from my Department Chair and was simply, "WTF?" But I found that the majority of the questions had to do with death and the afterlife. People wanted to know what happened to their loved ones (and to themselves) after they died. Was there an afterlife at all? If so, what was it like? Why did some seem to be taken so young or tragically? Would there be reward or punishment there?

I knew that many of my students were at the age when they were losing their grandparents, who often had been the ones at home with them while their parents worked. From the journals they kept for my classes and from personal conversations, I also understood how much death—of close friends and peer relatives—they had experienced due to drug abuse or drunk driving, much more than had been the case when I was younger. Questions of a possible afterlife, its nature and meaning, far outweighed any others in the survey.

Clearly the next step was to create some programming around these questions. But where to start? The vast majority of my school's population came from Christian backgrounds, primarily Roman Catholic, but other denominations as well. I knew from the Religious Studies courses I taught that they already had a basic knowledge of concepts such as Heaven, Hell, and Purgatory—and still their questions remained.

As previously mentioned, my partner in making any decisions of import is always my wife, The Lovely Christine (as my friends so rightly call her). This decision would be no exception.

Christine is a dyed-in-the-wool reincarnationist, holding firmly to the idea that we come back from each death as a new person, still with the memories and experiences of the people we had been, very present, beneath the surface. We'd spoken of this often. As a former Catholic and ex-seminarian, I'd been raised with the tripartite view of the afterlife, one shot resulting in eternal bliss or eternal misery, if perhaps with a stint in purgatorial circumstance. Now as a Renewal Jew (Judaism's most progressive form), the idea of a Hell had fallen away. Judaism generally does not concern itself with the afterlife, preferring to center on this life. There was no set or prescribed view regarding life after death; some believed in an eternal rest, others in the joy of unending Torah study in a Heavenly Academy. The idea of a Heaven or Paradise had seeped in from Christianity and Islam over the centuries. And Mystical Judaism, known as Kabbalah, did speak about reincarnation. One of the things I had come to love about Judaism was its non-dogmatism; as the saying went, "Two Jews, five opinions." And just about everyone seemed fine with that approach to things, including with regards to the afterlife.

As would prove to be the case over and over again, Christine provided me with just the impetus and insight to change my life drastically for the better! She took from her nightstand her well-worn copy of the book *Many Lives, Many Masters*, by Dr. Brian Weiss, and handed it to me.

I had always been ambivalent about reincarnation. "It's as plausible as any other theory of the afterlife, I suppose," I would say to my lovely wife. But this book intrigued me from its first pages. I read it in a weekend. It details the experiences of Dr. Weiss, a man of science and a skeptic, with a psychotherapeutic client he calls "Catherine." In treatment, Catherine seemed to remember past people, places, and events that she could not possibly have known. Reviewing these past lives seemed to be aiding in her therapeutic progress. Quite reluctantly at first, Dr. Weiss had to admit that a phenomenon known as "past-life regression" was occurring—a process through which, in an extremely relaxed state, a person could remember their previous incarnations. In an extension of the long held psychological premise that events from one's past (especially traumatic ones, blocked from conscious memory) impact one's present mental health, past-life therapy allows the treatment to delve even farther back, to see if the root of a problem may lie in a previous existence.

Mid-way through my reading of the book, I knew that this was a viewpoint on the afterlife that chaplaincy could present in response to the survey. I contacted the Weiss Institute in Florida, asking for any possible speakers in my area. From the list they graciously provided, I contacted Dr. Hammerman.

Sylvia, a welcoming, eloquent woman with a smile as genuine as her interest in others, was simply wonderful in her presentation to the audience of mostly students but which included faculty and staff as well. She detailed the process of regression and offered fascinating examples from her own work, always maintaining confidentiality. After the Q & A, I approached her; I was not looking for a therapist at that time, but would she consider leading a regression for me as a "spiritual exercise?" She enthusiastically agreed!

Now, in the seventh such session, each exploring the same past life, I found myself remembering a time and set of spiritual circumstances that had been lost to history, intentionally wiped from the communal memory of both Christians and Jews. It was the era before the split between the two, when the Jesus Movement was one of many sects of Judaism, and when Jews who believed in Jesus still considered themselves to be good, faithful Jews. And the person I had been, Yossi, the last Essene, was sitting in their Sabbath service.

WAYNE-DANIEL BERARD

Commentary from Sylvia

It is always enjoyable to connect with a bright, engaging individual who is open to the realm of reincarnation. So much of my professional experience has been with feet planted in two distinct arenas, the traditional psychology world and the therapy world, which is open to a spiritual dimension, including the experience of multiple lifetimes. For many years I felt the need to be discreet about this second area of interest, living in a rather conservative professional community where "spiritual" can be dismissed as hokey and "unscientific." Speaking with interested undergraduates was a breath of fresh air.

Then when Wayne-Daniel wanted to explore on his own I was certainly game. What I did not then know was how unique and engaging his regression experience would turn out to be.

First of all, he was a really good regression "subject" (the technical term for clients undergoing hypnosis). Smooth and easy. He was able to go deep quickly and connect with the place where he needed to go. Often the work of the regression therapist is to help move the client into the details and emotions of the narrative. In this case, I had to suggest to W-D to limit the details to what was important. His recall and attention to detail were phenomenal. Usually a past-life regression entails one, two, or three sessions tops to fully explore the lessons of a particular lifetime. With WD, this one lifetime took 12 sessions. And if I had not kept suggesting to limit the details I am sure it would have been another 3–4 sessions.

The other notable aspect of this work was the interesting nature of the context and content. I try to take fairly verbatim notes. There were many moments when my pen was flying and I felt mesmerized by what I was hearing, as if watching a really fascinating historical documentary.

At the same time, the goal was to be therapeutic, so I was listening for the material that had emotional meaning and would need special attention for the healing aspect of the work.

All in all, these were amazing sessions!

CHAPTER 3

Return of the Repressed

If, as St. John's Prologue insists, in the beginning was the word, in terms of 1st–2nd-century spirituality, that word was "diversity." This included Judaism; there were multitudinous ways to be Jewish, including a number whose members embraced Jesus of Nazareth in one way or another, while never considering themselves anything other than Jews. Ebionites, Cerinthians, Elcesaites, Nazarenes, and others all flourished during this period, each a sect of Judaism with what we might call a "Jesus component." If you haven't ever heard of most of them, this is not surprising. For as the 2nd Century CE progressed, its earlier pluralism did not. Exclusivism, the idea that there could be only One Truth and that any other views were dangerous if not damning, was coming to the fore. Soon, the culture at large would demand a choice: Were you a Jew or a Christian? You could no longer legitimately (or safely) be both.

At the root of this flight from inclusivity was the great enemy of human acceptance and multiculturalism—war.

THE LAST ESSENE

In 66 CE, thirty-three years after the death of Jesus and the birth of a Jesus Movement within Judaism, the Jewish people revolted against the Roman Empire. Although achieving some initial success, by 69 CE all that the rebels held was the Temple Mount in Jerusalem, but even this was divided among a splintered, self-competing resistance. Jerusalem fell in 70 CE; the Great Temple was destroyed, never to be rebuilt even to our own day. Jerusalem was a ruin. 600,000 Jewish lives were lost; one Jew of every three living in Judea was killed. Alexandria in Egypt, a polyglot community, and long an important center or Jewish life outside the Holy Land, now became *the* principle city in Jewry.

The power vacuum left by the defeat of the rebellion meant only one thing: an intense and vicious political struggle for the leadership and direction of whatever remained of Jewish life. A number of the factions that had survived, notably the Pharisee and Jesus Movements, went at each other's throats in ways to make our own fractured dialogue look like a love fest.

The time when one could be Jewish *and* have anything to do with Jesus or be involved with Jesus and *still* consider yourself a Jew was coming to an end. "Either-Or" was winning out over "Yes, and." In the Alexandria I was remembering via past-life regression, a city known for mutual acceptance and the cross pollination of a near infinite amount or peoples, religions, and spiritualities, "Yes, and" was still possible. But for how long?

The assiduous notes I kept after each session with Sylvia detail just such an expression of fragile spiritual openness and welcome:

At one point (in the service), someone started singing, and everyone joined in; I didn't know the song. It was in Greek. Some prayers were said in common. Then a woman got up from a bench, behind and to the left of the bima. Everything got very quiet; there was clearly a lot of respect for this woman. She went to the cabinet (the ark) and opened it; I was very surprised to see a woman doing this. But then two men came forward from the left and right. They each took one of the spool handles of the Torah, they turned and lifted the Torah a little and showed it to the people. It was tied shut with a piece of white cloth. People sang. Then the three of them went to the bima; the men unwrapped the cloth and rolled out the scroll. The woman then read/chanted the reading; it was in Greek, and talked about the Passover lamb (or goat), how to cook it, etc. I thought that at that point we'd all sit down, and she would give a little talk. But instead everyone sang the same song over again, but then the song changed. Everyone turned around, and a man walked down the center from the entrance with another scroll. This one was not as big or thick as the Torah scroll; he held it in front of him, open, by the lower end of the two spools. When he got to the front, the singing stopped, and the man read aloud. It was the account of the crucifixion of the Christos, his statements, etc. After he'd read, the song began again, and the man processed back the way he'd come. Then we all sat.

To my knowledge, there are no surviving accounts of Sabbath services for what I will call here, for lack of another name, "Christos Jews"—Jews who believed in Jesus and who saw themselves as one more streak of color in the variegated expression of faith that was Judaism. Now I was relating a first-hand experience of just such a service!

It had long been speculated (and often rejected) that the Christian gospels may have been written in such a way as to correspond to and converse with the Torah readings for Shabbat. Now I was seeing this play out before the eyes of my past-life memory.

It was very quiet for a few minutes. Then a man with a very gruff voice began speaking, saying that the Christos was the Passover lamb who had been sacrificed so the angel of death wouldn't come to "us, his followers." There were a few more seconds of quiet; then a woman on our side of the aisle said that she didn't agree; "How could God sacrifice God?" she said. It didn't make any sense to her. Almost immediately, a man from the other side of the aisle spoke up and said that the Christos wasn't God, but a very good man and a prophet. God had come into him and performed many miracles. But when the Christos was crucified, God's spirit had left him; that's why he said, "Why have you abandoned me?" God couldn't die, so he had to leave the Christos at that moment. Another man on our side said no, that the Christos was God and that God went through human life and death so that God could understand us fully. Another person, a woman, jumped in from the other side, saying that God was already all-knowing. It was getting to be a very nasty debate and reminded me of the Academy I and my master had escaped from. Things were getting very heated.

I was amazed at what my past-life memory was revealing! Here, at the beginning of the 2nd century CE, was a community of Jews who believed in Jesus, in which discussion of Scriptural passages, open to everyone, men *and* women, was the norm in a service. In true Jewish style, there was little agreement and things could get heated. But the mere fact that such discussion took place was monumental.

The woman then stood up and approached the bima. Everyone was quiet. She looked about 35–40, she was rather tall and wore a head cover. I leaned over and whispered to La'nah's mother, "Who is she?" She answered, "She's his daughter." I didn't know the Christos had a daughter. "Whose daughter?" I said. "John Mark's daughter," she answered. (John Mark was the author of Mark's Gospel).

The woman looked right at me and then at La'nah's mother. She said, "We have a distinguished guest with us, an Assah (Essene) from the desert, back home. I'd like to ask him to share any thoughts he has with us." I was stunned. Everyone in the place turned and looked at me! It got very hot in there! What should I do? If I said the wrong thing, it could jeopardize things with the mother. I said, "Thank you, but I'm not one of your group . . . yet. I'm only a guest, and don't feel I should speak." But the woman just nodded at me, as if to say, "Go on." So, I said, "I don't know much about your Christos, although everything I've heard has been favorable. I can't speak to who he may or may not be. But I do know one thing: The Lord God does not want anyone to suffer. He does not want anyone to sacrifice themselves. From what I know, your Christos tried to stop suffering and hurt, and called on his followers to do the same. As far as I can see it, his death was a crime. He was betrayed by the leadership, just as my people (the Essenes) were betrayed by the leadership. Leaders will sometimes do this, but we must not. No explanation or truth is worth hurting someone else. I think your Christos taught this, and because of this he is to be praised."

That was all. I could see La'nah looking at me with those big brown eyes, filled with admiration and love. There was a little quiet. Then everyone stood up for silent prayer. I wrapped my face in my tallit and prayed: "Please God—please no more alone. Please don't punish me if I take this girl. I can't be alone anymore. Help me to know this is the right thing. Tell me I've done enough. Let me be happy now—let it be true." I was crying a little into my tallit, (and also in the chair in the office).

One can see that, as important as the spiritual dynamic unfolding before me was, another aspect of my past-life regression, a far more personal one, was clearly every bit as important. Who was this La'nah? Why was she so central? Why did her mother's approval matter so much? What "master" and "Academy" was I remembering? For that matter, who was I?—Yosiah, Yossi, the "Essene from the desert," somehow thrown in with these people in ancient Alexandria? And why was I so afraid to be alone, yet so fearing God's punishment if I became anything else?

Perhaps it is time for this narrative to reveal its own past?

Commentary from Sylvia

As this narrative unfolds you will see that this is a story with many facets.

WAYNE-DANIEL BERARD

It is a story with an engaging storyline, full of drama, intensity, emotion, and action.

It is story with a fascinating context and historical breadth and depth.

It is a story that functions as a therapeutic vehicle, being the source of trauma, and untapped personal resource.

Finally, it is a story that holds meaning beyond itself, with universal lessons particularly relevant to our current world.

CHAPTER 4

"Remembering . . . is the beginning of always." —Dante

Session One

After doing quite a bit of background work, Dr. Hammerman asked if I wanted to try a regression with what was left of the time. I said yes, of course. Dr. Hammerman suggested using meditation, as that was already my practice. Once we began, she asked my "Higher Self" to lead me to that past life which would be most beneficial for me to experience in terms of my present situation, issues, etc. She likewise asked my Subconscious if it was alright to proceed. No hesitation surfaced. And so, we began.

At first, my meditation didn't go very deeply, until Dr. Hammerman began "counting me down the elevator floors." At one point, the "curtains parted"; I very clearly saw a room—I say "clearly," although the room itself was dark and beginning to fill up with smoke. The walls were curved, as if the building were round, and they were made of mustard-colored stone or mud brick. There were no windows. I had a sense of this scene being rather ancient. I was observing this, rather than being a part of it. In the lower left of my vision there was a man; he looked to be maybe late twenties/early thirties. He had a close-cropped but pointy dark beard, and wore a tunic type of thing, with a kilt bottom with fringe. The clothing looked dark blue or purple, but it was hard to make out with the lack of light and the smoke. Clearly the place was on fire; men were running about panicked, grabbing up long scrolls as if to save them. I could hear cries of pain, although they were somewhat distant, and also heard the sharp clang of metal upon metal.

In the center of this room was a big, circular open fireplace (imagine one of those big spools for cable you see out on the roads with construction crews—it looked somewhat like one of these, set on its end). The top surface of this fireplace was circular, and a rather large flame burned at its center. But I sensed nothing wrong with this; the fire belonged there and was not the cause of the smoke or panic. I could tell that this was a hot climate, but it was even more hot in the room; I could begin to see the shadows of flames against the round wall.

In the lower right of my vision, next to the man, I could see a boy (I saw no women or girls, only men and boys). He looked about 6 or 7 and was blonde. He was just standing there, looking at the fireplace, seemingly frozen, not knowing what to do. The man, who stood about four feet away to the boy's left and cradled two long scrolls, leaned toward him as if he were about to say something. That was the point at which Dr. Hammerman began to lead me out of the meditation.

THE LAST ESSENE

I have rarely ever been so deep in the meditative state. Remnants of it remained for most of the day.

This began the most amazing adventure of my life, one that I did not need to leave an armchair in an office to have. I remember having a terrible cold that day and, even though Sylvia was very patient and able, I was not getting anywhere at first in terms of seeing or sensing any past-life memories. I was just about to say, "Let's try again when I'm feeling better," when suddenly the curtains before my inner eye parted, and I saw (and heard) the scene described above. I had absolutely no idea what I was looking at, what this place might be or who these men were. Neither did I recognize the little blonde boy, frozen in panic before the raised firepit. Some sort of catastrophe was clearly ensuing, but I was clueless as to what I might be.

When I've related these and further past-life experiences to others, I'm often asked the same set of questions: How do I know that this was not just my imagination? Could it have been a "waking dream?" And (most affronting of all) wasn't this just a case of my "wanting it to be true," of wanting so much for reincarnation and past-life memory to be real that my psyche merely fulfilled that wish?

I don't know how to answer these questions except by relying on direct experience: I'm a writer. I have a very vivid imagination and have created entire fantasy worlds for my novels and short stories.

I know what that looks like and feels like, and most of all, I always know that these are *fiction*. What I was experiencing in Sylvia's office was an extremely vivid set of *memories*, similar in feel and scope to any other memories that I might have at any time—memories of something *real*, of events that had actually happened. No imagination, no matter how fertile, could have possibly produced something so definitely *remembered* rather than *created*.

The same is true for dreams, waking or otherwise. Often, I have emerged from a dream saying to myself, "Wow, how real that was!" But I'd have no doubt, once I'd awakened, that it had been a dream. By the same token, I'd never had to ask myself, upon remembering, if the memory were actually a dream (although I have, like most of us, had instances of remembering a dream hours or days afterwards).

No, imaginings and dreams were apples, and memories were oranges—there was simply no comparison.

As for "wish fulfilment," all I could say is that I honestly had no interest at all in what forms, if any, an afterlife might take. If anything, having an actual past-life experience would mean I might have to admit to the Lovely Christine that she'd been right about something I'd sort of pooh-poohed when she'd brought it up to me! So, if anything, wish-fulfillment here would have gone the other way!

THE LAST ESSENE

I had set off on this experiment because I was, and had always been, a seeker, and not one content to merely seek through reading or classes. I wanted to *experience* things for myself, to draw my own conclusions. That, and I certainly did not want to expose, through a chaplaincy presentation, something to my community that I wasn't willing to try myself.

And so, I came away from my first past-life regression session with no doubt that what I'd experienced was real, but with no idea what I'd actually experienced!

I scheduled a second session for the following week.

Commentary from Sylvia—a bit about the process

Wayne-Daniel's questions about the nature of his unfolding story are typical of most regression experiencers. People often ask: How do I know this is "real"? Is it memory or my creation?

He didn't raise these questions with me during the time of our sessions, but I'm not surprised to learn that he had them and needed to come to some resolution in order to proceed. I learn from this reading that W-D was remarkably adept at processing through his questions by comparing his felt experience of all the possibilities—memory, fantasy, wish fulfillment, dreams, coming to a conclusion that relied heavily on instinct, tempered with thoughtful, rational considerations.

Well done, Wayne-Daniel! If he had brought up this concern in the session, I would have offered a more simple opening to the same pathway, something like: "We don't really know if it is 'real' but what is real is the emotion that is evoked in you, your emotional connection to this story.

See if you can ask the rational, logical part of you to step aside and allow the process to unfold without censoring or questioning for now. Perhaps this logical part can wait until later to assess the accuracy and usefulness of what you are about to learn."

Interestingly, in my own session notes, after this first session I wrote: "remarkable connection and resonance".

And the "connection and resonance" were far from over!

Years after these sessions had concluded, I had the opportunity to visit Israel and decided to make certain I went to Qumran and walked through its ruined Essenic compound.

I was staying at a monastery on Mt. Zion where I met another seeker who became a fast friend. Fred was a Catholic educator from Kentucky, with a particular thirst to get to know the Jewish Jesus. This longing had brought him to The Holy Land, and we engaged in many memorable conversations for the both of us.

THE LAST ESSENE

One morning, as I was setting off from the guest house for the bus station and Qumran, I ran into Fred. Asking where I was headed, he volunteered to accompany me, explaining that I would probably need some guidance maneuvering the complicated "bus situation" (apparently one system for Arabs, one system for Jews). I'd had no idea. Fred had already been to Qumran on a previous trip, and I was thrilled for the pleasant and knowledgeable company.

On the fifty-minute ride, Fred asked me why I was heading to Essenic ruins. Was it an academic interest? I laughed and replied, "You may want to stop the bus and get away from the crazy man after I tell you this, but here goes!" I related to him my experience in regression, my past-life as Yossi, and much of what all this had revealed and come to mean to me. Fred replied, without missing a beat, that he was "honored to share this journey" with me.

The bus pulled into the historic site; it was blisteringly hot out and the long, silver line of the Dead Sea spread itself in the distance. We paid our twenty shekels and approached the actual ruins, a collection of low, mustard-colored limestone walls and crisscrossing walkways.

"We go in here," I said, moving toward a break in the wall.

"That says, 'Exit,'" Fred pointed out.

"That may be what it says," I replied, "but this is where we went in."

I remembered everything.

The saying, "Muscle has memory" must apply to past-life memory as well. Without any conscious direction on my part, my feet knew exactly where to go.

I was giving my new friend a 1st-century tour of the Essenic compound at Qumran!

"This is where we ate," I said. "There would be blankets spread out across the ground. The men would eat first; we boys would wait on them. Then we would eat after." As we turned a corner, there was a sign reading "Refectory," with a drawing of men sitting on blankets, eating.

"And this, "I continued, as we walked along "is where the scrolls were written. Scribes would lean over stone lecterns, writing. We boys would stand with our backs to the wall, hands clasped behind us. If someone called out for "Ink!" or "Reed! we would hurry to provide them. (The scribes wrote with a hollow, pointed reed).

Just then we arrived at the room marked "Scriptorium."

"But where is the round, raised fireplace I saw in my first regression?" I asked. "It should be right around here someplace?"

"Wayne-Daniel, look down," Fred said softly.

There at my feet were a series of concentric circles of stone, imbedded into the earth.

As we moved along, I unthinkingly retraced my escape route from the Scriptorium toward the compound's wall. I noted to Fred the stone cistern dug into the ground, and the water route running toward a low opening in the wall. "That is where I crawled out," I explained. "It was hot, and the channel was dry."

We picked our way over the stones out into the area between the compound and the barren Judaean hills. These is where I had scrambled up to escape the destruction of my home. I could now see (and remember) several caves; as a later memory would reveal to me, in one of these I had been born and my mother had died giving birth to me.

There were signs everywhere in a variety of languages warning travelers of the loose footing and forbidding them to climb any further. But I hadn't come this far to be daunted now! I started up one of the hills, until I heard Fred's voice close to begging me not to continue. "I don't want to have to call your Christine," he pleaded in his smooth drawl, "and tell her you're in an Israeli hospital with a broken leg!" Reluctantly, I listened.

I already knew all I needed to know.

CHAPTER 5

Who are you? Who are your people? Where do you come from?

Session Two

(one week later)

Dr. Hammerman led me into meditation, seeking for me to return to that same place and time. As with the first session, nothing happened initially, and I began to worry that it might be a bust this time. Then, the deeper I got, I began to notice a swirling sort of disc shape, forming out of the usual dips and forms that one sees when one's eyes are closed. It struck me as being something like a burning sun; then—zap!—it was a sun, very hot, overlooking a desert scene. Then, suddenly, the scene shifted to back in the original room. But this time, I was seeing things through the eyes of the boy I described previously. He was terrified and confused. The man leaned forward and told him very forcefully to run, to run fast and not to stop until he was far away. (Actually, I couldn't make out the actual words the man said, but that was the meaning that I knew they had). I began to run. I was a little kid with short legs, in a sort of tannish, nondescript tunic, about knee-length. There was a hall leading from the room, and an arched door at the end of it. I pushed it open and was outside, behind the round building. It stood just back from center of some kind of compound. The place was clearly under attack. Men were running, shouting. Buildings were on fire. Everything was pandemonium. I ran toward the rear of the compound, toward a little grating in the wall; I'd say it was about two/two-and-a-half-feet tall. I knew that this was where the water came in, but it was dry now. The grate had two metal rods running through its left and right sides into the ground; I pulled them up and moved the grate aside. I got down on my hands and knees; I barely fit through the opening. The ground felt like dry clay against my hands, knees, and shins.

There was no grating on the other side; the back wall looked out onto an expanse of about thirty yards, followed by a high hill, that looked like a glacier in stone—lots of rills, no trees or grass. I began to climb up on my hands and knees; the surface was pumicey and somewhat slippery. I'd slide back a bit every now and then. When I'd look back and down, I could see the compound. It was surrounded on three sides by attackers. I could see fire coming from many of the buildings; ancient-looking soldiers with straps of metal or leather across their chests and helmets on their heads were trying to scale the walls on makeshift ladders. Other soldiers were on horseback, riding back and forth, seeming to give orders; they had red cloaks and red bristles on the top of their helmets. Over to the far side were soldiers dressed differently; they had helmets with a sort of curlicue crest on them. They were darker skinned and shot flaming arrows into the compound. I'd stop to watch; this was my home, the only home I'd known. I wanted to help; I felt like I should do something! Then I remembered that "Avel" had said to run and to keep running—this was the first time I had a name for the man. He was in charge of me and the other boys *who lived in the compound. I liked Avel very much and wanted to do what he told me. So, I kept climbing. At the top, I lay flat on my stomach and looked down. Now the soldiers were in the compound. I could see sword's flashing in the sun and people writhing, falling. I was afraid to stand up, afraid the soldiers might see me. I could see that my home was gone and that everything and everyone I knew was gone. (I actually began to cry there in the chair). I crawled away a bit, then got up and ran as fast as I could. Pretty soon, it was downhill; I slipped and slid and scraped my bare legs. When I got to the bottom, I had no idea what to do or where to go. I decided to just follow the sun and start walking. (The thought came to me that "we pray with the sun every morning"). It was past noon, and the sun was heading west. I just began walking.*

Dr. Hammerman had given me specific instructions. "I know you're an academic," she'd said, "but I want you *not* to do any research on what you're remembering—not yet, anyway." I had followed her wishes, and so still had no idea about the historical background of the scenes I was reliving in memory. The only sense I had was that they were ancient in character.

A significant difference between this session and the last involved perspective. In that first regression, I had observed what was going on as if it were a movie or TV show. This time, the perspective had switched; now I *was* the little boy, remembering his experiences first-hand. The sense-memory was astonishing; I *felt* the heat of that desert sun and the smudge of the caked clay on my hands and knees; I *heard* the moans of those being killed by the invaders. Although I never lost touch with the fact that this was a memory, it was definitely a first-person experience!

Commentary by Sylvia

I have a distinct memory of wanting to make sure W-D did not contaminate the unfolding process with historical information. I already sensed that his direct experience would lead to something very personally important. I knew we did not want to compromise that in any way.

By the second session, W-D had switched to a first-person accounting, rather than the observer perspective of session one. This is a sign of being embodied and fully present with the experience. He has given himself permission to "go there" and is getting comfortable feeling it is safe to do that. There is a fine balance that must be reached to encourage this full embodiment while ensuring that the client is not overwhelmed with strong emotion. Perhaps the suggestion I usually make at the beginning of the work helps with this: "There is always a part of you present who knows you are here in this room remembering. Even if it's a tiny speck on your shoulder, it is always there." It is rather amazing that the unconscious mind takes suggestions like that to heart.

The boy I was in this memory was a bit chubby, maybe 6–7 years old, with blonde hair extending in ringlets down each side of his face. He was a very trusting child, especially so of Avel, whom he knew as his caregiver and that of other boys in the compound. This child was anxious to follow Avel's instruction.

I was also amazed at the composure, almost the matter-of-factness, with which this boy whom I had been faced his new circumstances. The only home he had ever known was being destroyed before his eyes; everyone he knew, including Avel, was facing annihilation. And he was utterly alone at 6 or 7 years old, just walking off into a barren desert. This boy possessed a remarkable sense of composure—or was it just that he was too young to know any better?

I walked and walked. I told myself that I was a good walker, that I could keep going. I'd never been but a few yards away from the compound before. I had no idea what was out here. I was very thirsty, but there was no stream or anything. I just kept walking; the area was all dirt and stones and a few scrub trees. I didn't let myself stop; Avel had said to keep going, so I kept going. After a while the sun began to set; it was getting cold. I didn't know what to do. I saw a flat, rectangular rock and lay down on it, although I told myself I had to stay awake, in case animals came in the night. I was so scared and cold, hungry and thirsty. I must have fallen asleep, because at one point it was very early morning. I was so cold. I stood up, faced the other way toward the sun, and tried to put myself in a state of prayer. I turned toward the sun and swayed and tried to pray but didn't known the words to the morning prayers. I was too young to have them taught to me, and the children were not allowed to pray along with the rows of men, but just observed. I did my best, then started walking, keeping the sun behind me. I was incredibly thirsty and very hungry, but I had to keep walking. At one point, I stopped to rest. I decided to "practice my strokes" in the dirt with my finger. Avel was going to teach me to write, but first I had to have the strokes and flourishes down exactly. After a time, I got back up and kept walking. I was so tired and thirsty; my tongue felt like an old, dry piece of sponge in my mouth. Finally, I started to see some little tufts of grass here and there, then a few more. When the sun started going down, I settled myself in among three of four tufts. I was so thirsty and cold, but I still fell asleep. The next thing I knew, I was awake in the morning and thought I heard a noise. I tried to walk in its direction; it got louder, and I could tell it was lots of steps and the bleating of animals. I came up upon a flock sheep or goats, I don't know which. They were brown and black with floppy ears and looked different from sheep or goats I'd seen in "this current" life. Anyway, I figured they must be going somewhere, where there might be water(!) I came up on the back of the flock and ducked down as I walked; I didn't want to be caught. I walked among the sheep/goats, all hunched over for quite a while; my back hurt. The animals made my nose itch (in the chair, I actually started scratching!) I moved forward in the flock and could see a person up toward the front. It took me a minute to realize that this was a woman; I'd never seen a woman. They weren't allowed in the compound. She had on a long, sort of maroon robe with a rope or woven belt, and she was veiled with a head cover. She carried a staff. I didn't want her to see me, but I really needed water.

More clues! Whatever that compound was in which I'd been raised, it clearly had a religious character, and a somewhat unorthodox one—*"we prayed in the direction of the sun."* The community seemed to possess some sort of a school—only for boys—in which they were taught to read and write (skills that the vast majority did not possess in that day). And the boy that I was had never seen a woman before; they were forbidden from the compound!

But all that was about to change.

Soon we came to a sort of corral made out of stones with rails across an opening. I had hoped to sneak in with the flock, then make my way toward water (hopefully) at night. But at the opening, she saw me. She called out, sounding angry. She held onto my right arm and pinned the staff against my left arm. She asked me what my name was, who my people were, and where I came from (again, I couldn't understand the actual words, but knew this was what I was being asked). I did not like her touching me, and worried that she might be "unclean." I raised myself up as tall as I could and tried to speak, but my mouth was just parched. I coughed, and she repeated the questions. Finally, I said that my name was "Yossi—Yosiah." I said that I was "Assah," although I really wasn't one yet; I was too young. But I said it anyway. I didn't know what to say about "where I came from." We had just called the compound "The Place." Even with the veil, I could see that she was smiling, and I felt indignant. I thought that this woman was laughing at me. She told me to follow; I didn't like this, but I did it. Just a few steps away from the corral was a sort of stone lean-to, three walls, open on one side, with pieces of scrub trees laid out for a roof. She brought me inside; there was a blanket laid out on the left side of the dirt floor. She told me that she slept with the sheep, but I could stay here. She gave me what my "conscious self" recognized as a water skin, but the "me" in the scene had never seen one before and didn't know how to operate it. Water spilled onto me, and I was embarrassed, but too thirsty to care much. Then the woman left. I thought I would just lay down on the blanket and sleep a bit, then run off before she could come back in the morning. The blanket was gray and somewhat rough, but I could wrap myself in it.

Just before falling asleep, scenes of life in the compound ran through my head. There were about 12–15 boys who lived there. We had our own sleeping quarters, on mats on the floor. Avel would come before dawn and wake us; we would file out in silence and stand behind the men as they prayed while the sun rose. Then we would go to a pool with three steps leading into it at one end and three more leading out at the other. We would strip down to the cloths wrapped around our hips and crotch, and Avel would go in with each of us one at a time. It was cold in the mornings! He'd say prayers and we'd dip in three times. After coming out, we'd put our tunics on over our wet under cloth, run back to our sleeping quarters and change our under cloth. Then we'd quietly go to meal in the dining hall; some of us served the meal to the men. We boys sat on benches at a table over to one side and were always served last, by one of the older boys. I recalled how quiet and peaceful The Place was, and how much I liked that.

At this point, I fell asleep wrapped in the blanket in the lean-to. This was the point when Dr. Hammerman began to lead me out of the meditation.

"Curiouser and curiouser," as Alice said. But some pieces were beginning to clarify themselves.

There was my fear of and condescension toward women. I worried that the goatherd who touched me might be "unclean"—plus I was not at all pleased at being led by a woman.

Then there were my "memories within a memory," particularly that of a ritual bath that we boys who lived in the compound seem to take each morning.

The final clue in this particular regression came in the form of my name in that lifetime: "Yossi, short for Yosiah." That, and the name "Avel" seemed to leave little doubt.

The uncleanness the boy I had been seemed to fear had to be the ritual uncleanness detailed in the Torah (especially as regards woman and menstruation). The bath could only be a mikveh, the immersion used for ritual purity or to demonstrate repentance.

And my ancient name, Yossi, short for Yosiah, was clearly Hebrew. "Yosiah" means "God will save" (Jesus' own name, *Yeshua*, is a variant of this). And *Avel* is the Hebrew name rendered "Abel" in English, as in "Cain and Abel."

I had come to my present Jewishness through the long and circuitous route of an adoption search, which finally had revealed my Jewish birth family. Pursuing that connection had led me to Torah study, to an immersion in Jewish life, to becoming part of a Jewish Renewal community—in short, to a full and very joyous self-identification as a Jew.

Now I was seeing that my essential Jewishness ran even deeper than that. The woman who had saved me from dying in the desert had asked me three questions, perhaps the most basic three questions of all: Who was I? Who were my people? And where I had come from? In all three cases, the answers had been Jewish.

As the great Israeli poet Yehuda Amicai has written in his poem *The Jews,*

And there are pictures restored from old yellowing

    photographs.

And sometimes people come and break the window

And burn the pictures. And then they begin

To photo anew and develop anew

And display them again aching and smiling.

It seemed that in my present I had been developing and displaying a Jewishness that for me was both very new and very old.

In my seat in Sylvia's office, I both ached and smiled.

CHAPTER 6

A School of Becoming

Session 3

(the following week)

In this session, it took me a shorter time to reach the past life, although it seemed that I was not meditating as deeply as during the previous two sessions.

Again, I was seeing everything through the eyes of the little boy, Yossi. I am now living with the shepherd woman (or goatherd?), and with another boy (Dothan) and girl (Ruth). Dothan is increasingly angry at my presence in the house; the little girl, however, enjoys me, and I her. Almost nothing seems to be expected of me. In the morning, the woman (whom the other two children call "Amma") leaves for the day, presumably to look after the flock. She takes Dothan with her; I'm left at the house with Ruth, I'd imagine to take care of her. We play outside (hide and seek). When the boy comes back at the end of the day, he glares at me. On one occasion, I'm practicing my strokes in the dirt floor with a stick; Dothan walks by and rubs them out with his foot.

The woman seems somewhat aloof from all of us. I'm not sure if these are her birth children or if she is just caretaking them. I never see her hug or kiss them, and she never does these to me either, but she does seem fine with Ruth climbing on her lap or clinging to her robe from behind.

We sleep at night on the roof of the house. On the left side, as you enter, there's a sloping ladder, with which we climb to an opening in the ceiling and out onto the flat roof. Around the edge of the roof is a slight rise, about six inches tall, so I don't worry about rolling off. We sleep on mats; Amma and Ruth on one side nearer the ladder; Dothan and I on the other. I rise as soon as the light begins to break and try to say the morning prayers, facing the sun, as we used to do in The Place. I do look over my shoulder a lot, as I don't trust Dothan not to shove me over the edge. But he's always still asleep.

One evening, when we go up to sleep, I see that my mat is missing. I feel certain that Dothan has thrown it off the roof, just for spite. Amma sees this and says that we must share the one mat, which really pisses off Dothan. We lie down; Dothan and I are back-to-back. Shortly, I feel an elbow in my kidneys, and edge farther away. Almost immediately I feel a heel kick me in the calf. Now I'm entirely off the mat, and I'm feeling very angry. So much has happened already, and I'm fed up with Dothan. So far, I have never laid a hand on him, trying to follow our rule about never attacking, but only defending ourselves. Erasing lines in the dirt didn't constitute an attack, I didn't *think, but now I'm being kicked and elbowed. I'm just on the verge of deciding what to do when Sylvia asks me to stop for a minute. She asks my "Higher Self" if there is anything still to come of significance in this past life; I respond by raising the index finger of my left hand, indicating "yes." Sylvia then asks me if any of the others in the life seem familiar or significant. She says that there may not be any physical resemblances to people in my present life, but urges me to "look in their eyes," presumably for a certain cast of expression and basic demeanor that I may recognize.*

This Amma gives me the feel of an archetypal female, the wise, spiritual woman— somewhat aloof, watching and caretaking overall.

The boy Dothan I don't get a sense of right away, but on the ride home, I recall his expression as being very like that of my maternal half-brother, Robert, when he saw me for the one and only time, across the cathedral at our mother's funeral. As for Ruth, there is something about her that reminds me a lot of the foster child we had in our home for four years (before she was returned to her mother). Her name was Denise, and we were and still are very close.

I get the strong idea that my time in this house and with these people is temporary. I'm looking forward greatly to the next session; I want to know what happens between Yossi and Dothan (I've always been violence-averse; the very idea of my fist hitting someone else's flesh made—and makes—my skin crawl. I'm wondering if this is rooted back there somehow?) I likewise would like to know where, if anywhere, I go next.

So much to consider here—particularly the notion of "past-life recognition."

Dr. Weiss and others point out that we tend to cycle through our incarnations with the same set of people important to our lives. Not each of them will necessarily be in each lifetime, but they will recur across the spectrum of our incarnations. They will appear differently each time, of course; they (and we) might be the father in one life or the mother in another, a wife or husband, child, friend, lover, etc. Often, we have unresolved issues with such people or a "karmic debt" that must be paid (more on this later). Or they may be just the right person to help us to grow in a particular way that we need, a companion, teacher, or mentor.

This leads us to an overarching question: Why reincarnation at all? What is the purpose, if any, of this consonant process of rebirth?

Among the concluding words in Brian Weiss' *Many Lives, Many Masters* are these:

We have lessons to learn in this school called Earth. We need to comprehend completely the concepts of compassion, love, non-violence, non-judgment, non-prejudice, generosity, charity, and hope. We need to recognize the deceptions and traps of the ego and to transcend them.

THE LAST ESSENE

We must become aware of the interconnectedness of all living things, that energy connects us all, and that there is no death, only life.

These lessons are vast and deep, and it seems we need many, many lifetimes, teachers, and companion students to learn them.

Additionally, the key lesson that I took away from my years of Torah study with my great teacher, Alan Ullman, comes to the fore here.

In Exodus, Chapter 3, Moses asks God, who is speaking to him from a burning bush, for God's name. Names in the ancient world were much more than just identifiers; one's name bespoke the essential nature of the person, who they truly were, the determining trait or event in their life. This was the case for Gods as well as people; the sky God of ancient Greece was called Zeus, which means "sky shaker." His weapon was the thunderbolt. The name of the ancient Egyptian Goddess Isis means "throne," and she was considered the divine mother of Pharaoh. Moses' own name means, "taken from the water," which fits his story perfectly.

So then, when Moses asks for God's name, he is really asking, "Who are you?"

God's response (here in transliterated Hebrew) is *Ehyeh-Asher-Ehyeh*. This is often translated "I Am Who Am," or "I Am That I Am." But ancient Hebrew is a very interesting language; it has *no present tense of the verb*. One cannot say "Am" in Biblical Hebrew. This phrase is in future tense, and literally means "I Will Be Whatever I Will Be."

In other words, this God is a *verb*, not a noun, not a person, place, or thing. Even more unusual, God is a verb in the future tense, indefinite. "I *Will* Be *Whatever* I *Will* Be."

Put another way, the God of Torah (and thus the God of Jesus and Christianity) is a *process*—a process of God's becoming whatever God will be!

And it seems that this God is an *indefinite* process, as well, becoming whatever that process might become. God cannot be anticipated or pinned down; one can never say "Never" with a process of becoming, nor can one say "Always." Only that the process of *Godding*—of God becoming God—is always ongoing and never completed.

And here was the moment from those studies that truly floored me—and elevated me at the same time.

According to that same Book, I (and everyone else) is made in the image and likeness of this very God.

Did I realize what that meant?

That if God were a verb, so was I.

That if God were a process of becoming God, then I, too was a process—of becoming myself.

And if that process of God's becoming was always ongoing and never completed, then the same applied for me.

By virtue of being alive, I was enrolled in this school called Earth. My major? *Selfing*! Avel and the goatherd, Dothan and Ruth, were among my teachers in this Program of Becoming. And just as remembering what was learned in preceding grades is essential to the next ones, my past-life memories of Yossi would promote my own Process of Becoming in ways I could not even imagine—of course not! I Would Be *Whatever* I Would Be!

CHAPTER 7

Across the Universe

Session Four

It had been two weeks since the last session, and my biggest question involved what action the boy, Yossi, might have taken in terms of the other boy, Dothan. When Sylvia had brought me out of the meditation last session, Yossi was trying to decide whether to retaliate against the other boy elbowing and kicking him as he tried to sleep on the roof. I remember feeling, as Yossi, extremely angry and frustrated with Dothan. Over the weeks since the session, I'd been asking myself if perhaps my own pacifism, something that had been with me since childhood, might have originated here? I was kind of concerned— what if in that past life I'd done something in my anger to hurt Dothan or worse? (how far a drop was it from that roof?) What if I seemed born with strong non-violent tendencies in this life because in a past life I'd done something awful?

When the session started, I sank very deep into meditation; still, nothing seemed to be appearing in my field of vision. We (Sylvia,

THE LAST ESSENE

Christine, and myself) spent a good two-three minutes sitting in silence. Once again, I began to worry that nothing was going to happen. In the lower right of the "screen," there was a sort of dark, amorphous, twisting, turning, elongated form. I centered my attention there, and then the "curtain parted." I could see that the form was really myself (Yossi) and Dothan. We were wrestling in the pitch dark. I had my arms and legs wrapped around him from behind. Then the point of view shifted, and I was no longer observing this but participating. Dothan was writhing and wriggling. He was shouting as loud as he could for me to stop, to let him go. He called me what I knew were awful names (although I couldn't understand them). For my part, I just held on. The woman, over on the other side of the flat roof, did nothing and said nothing.

I asked Dothan if he would stop if I released him. He just cursed me louder and continued writhing. At one point he put his chin down and tried to bite my right upper arm, but couldn't get much of an angle (still, I felt the attempt right there in the chair). I asked him continually if he'd leave me alone if I let him go. Finally, he said yes. I asked him to give me his "word in Yah." Once again, he said yes. I let him go, fully expecting him to turn on me. But he didn't; he just stayed with his back to me and said nothing. In a few seconds, however, I could hear him crying, and I could see in the dark his form shuddering. I think I shamed him.

The scene changed. I felt that it was a day or two, maybe three, later. I was alone in the house with the little girl; we were sitting on the dirt floor by the unlit fire ring, and I was showing her how to make the strokes in the dirt with a stick. The curtain that served as the door opened and the woman came in with a man (no other boy). The man was shorter than she was and a little stooped. He had a sharp beard and leaned on a stick. They both stood there looking at me. The woman told me that I would be leaving with the man.

"When?" I asked. "Now," she said. I couldn't believe it. I felt like I was being punished for the incident with Dothan. I didn't want to go. I really liked the little girl, and this had become a home of sorts for me. The man stepped closer to me and said, "So you're the Assah from the desert." I stood up, as tall as I could and looked right into his face but said nothing. The man told me he had a school, that I was going to study. He looked at my strokes in the dirt floor. I asked if there were any others "like me" at the school. He said no, there were no more Assah; they were "all gone." I should "forget all about that," he said. I said nothing, but inside told myself that I would never forget, that I would stay who I was.

Then the man said to say goodbye. I got down on my right knee and told Ruth that I had to leave with this man. She said, "Where are you going?" I said that I was going to a school but promised that I would come back and see her. But inside I knew I would never come back. I felt awful that I would break my word to the little girl. Then I stood up, went to the woman and wrapped my arms around her. I pressed my cheek against her stomach; I wanted her to say I could stay, to tell me she wanted me there. But she didn't say anything; she just patted my shoulders, like a signal to let go. So, I did; the man turned and walked through the door. The woman held the curtain open. I followed him and never looked back.

THE LAST ESSENE

The man's name, I somehow knew, was Ishmael. I walked just behind him down the dirt road. I saw burnt out and abandoned buildings. After a while, the road dipped to the right between two hills. At this point, my frame of reference changed. I was now observing the bent little man and the boy walking away; then they passed behind the hills, and that was all.

The idea of past-life recognition seems to loom larger and larger as these regressions proceed.

I would come to recognize a number of people in present life who had been a part of my past life. Sometimes they would even look alike; at times it was the eyes that truly sealed that recognition for me. But just as often, it was what I would call the "emotional signature" between us that would be the most telling.

If we were to think for a moment of two people whom we know very well but who are *very* different from each other, I am willing to bet that each person, each relationship, would have its own emotional signature. How it feels, how *we* feel, to be with the one person compared to the other is incredibly distinct and personal, and they with us. We would recognize that feeling anywhere; it is the signature of our "I-Thou," and it is unmistakable.

The first person I recognized from my past life as Yossi was a woman in my Jewish Renewal community, who I knew immediately had been Amma, the goatherd who had sheltered and cared for me. I did not know her well, but shortly after that second regression session, I happened to be at a prayer event at which she was present. The moment she walked into the room, I knew who she had been; her tall, dignified carriage, her self-possessed but open manner. I felt the emotional signature of Yossi and Amma as clearly as I did with anyone in my present life. Unmistakable. (Luckily, this woman is a very openminded and openhearted person, who received with interest and, I think, joy, our conversation about past life).

Dothan and Ruth were people whom I recognized immediately, while still in the regression. The fact that we were family to each other in both lives is hardly unusual, when we consider the overarchingly important role family plays in any life, at any time. In this case, Denise/Ruth was also a very major part of my present-life's childhood, as the foster sister I loved dearly and who, truth be told, was a heart-relief in terms of the difficult relationship with my brother, two years younger than me, my adoptive parents' birthchild. After her birthmother was re-awarded custody of Denise, it had been difficult for me at twelve to maintain our relationship across time and distance. But as I became an adult, Denise and I reconnected and are very close to this day. In regression, I could see that, in my present life, I had been able to repair the broken promise that a very young Yossi had made to Ruth to return to her one day.

As for Dothan, I recognized him right away as my birth-brother, Robert. I had only seen him once, at my birthmother's funeral. I had found her only three months before; it was she who told me of my Jewishness. (She herself was Azorean Portuguese, but with a maiden name very common among Conversos, Jews who had been forced in the 15th century to convert to Christianity, go into exile, or be executed). My birthfather, who was from a Romanian Jewish family, had not been her husband, and had disappeared from my mother's life shortly after I was born. I had met two of my siblings from this family, a brother and sister, but Robert, the eldest, had refused.

At my birthmother's funeral Mass, I arrived early and took a nondescript seat in the back. I had not attended the wake, nor did I wish to assert some place in the family funeral procession. I feared that very quickly "the boy she gave away" could become the center of attention, and this, I understood, would have been very wrong. The focus needed to be on my birthmother and the family she had raised and loved, and who loved her. There would be other times for anything else.

As the family entered the church behind the casket, everyone stood. My new-found sister caught my eye and smiled; I saw her pull at the elbow of a man next to her and say something to him. He turned toward me; never in my life before or since had I seen such an expression of unbridled hostility, even hatred. "What had I done to him?" I wondered to myself.

Now, having remembered our experience together in the 1st century CE, I could better understand his animosity. As Dothan, he had been there first, and then along came this other boy, a member, though young, of the esteemed Essene community, someone who could at least begin to read and write. And worse, this avowed pacifist boy had subdued him in as non-violent a manner as possible and had extracted his promise in God to back off! Dothan had felt, I was certain, threatened by my existence and humiliated by my "victory" over him.

I was not sure what Robert in the late 20th century was feeling when he glared at me across that church. We never did meet, never talked together. But my regression experience left me certain that he was, in part at least, the victim of feelings sourced in an earlier life, just as experiences buried in childhood can impact adult feelings and behaviors, the cause of which is a complete mystery to the sufferer.

Robert died a number of years ago, but I have no doubt that our karmic entanglement is not over. I fully expect to see him again.

All of this only served to strengthen my certainty that what I was remembering was indeed a past life. If I were merely projecting from some unfulfilled need, the easiest thing would have been to see Dothan as the brother with whom I had actually grown up, and with whom I had had a difficult relationship. But there was never even a hint of that; instead, I clearly recognized this ancient presence in my life as someone I knew not at all in this one. Fiction would have been neater and tidier; real lives never are.

And then there was Avel.

THE LAST ESSENE

The celibate Essenes had no children but would take in and raise orphans. Avel was the man in charge of caring for these boys, and he saved my life that horrific day by urging me to run from the compound and not look back. (In later sessions, I would learn that Avel had been much more to me than just a teacher and caregiver). But almost immediately I recognized him as a very important figure in my present life.

I first met Bill over thirty-five years ago. Like many would-be academics, I was teaching part-time at any college I could commute to; I supplemented this with work at my local Catholic parish. I did everything from janitorial duties to program planning, my seminary experience coming in quite handy in both instances (I wish we could say we'd been liberated in our thinking, ahead of our time, but with virtually no women allowed on the grounds, all the housekeeping fell to us!) Bill's mother was the cook and housekeeper at the rectory, and he would stop by occasionally to see her. We struck up a friendship; we were both on the spiritual search. Bill would end up walking with me through some of the most difficult and the most joyous days of my life; no matter his own opinion of my changes and choices, he was right there, providing unconditional support and love. He was and is to this day my closest male friend, more of a brother than anything else.

When the time came for me to embark on my adoption search, Bill was invaluable. A historian and archivist, he guided me through the labyrinthine approaches involved with trying to find information on a "closed adoption." This designation meant that all records were sealed, and no information could be accessed by anyone, without an outstanding medical reason (which, thankfully, I lacked). Even with Bill's help, I had been at this for two years without results. I was ready to give up.

Then, one fateful Friday afternoon, I was about to head home from the college where I had finally landed a tenure-track position. It was early May and the term was almost over; I was running on fumes, as the saying goes. I decided to go right from my classroom to my car. As I passed the faculty office building, I heard my name being called through an open window. The faculty secretary (who did not care for me!) was trying to get my attention. At that point in my week and semester, I did not wish to stop to hear something else that I might have done wrong in her eyes. Determining to save that experience for Monday, I kept walking.

Soon I heard the quick, sharp *click, click, click* of heels on the sidewalk behind me. I was being pursued, my name still being sounded in a very distinct tone! I'm sure I turned with a look of impatience on my face.

My pursuer held out a piece of notepaper to me. "This call came for you, but I don't know what it means?" (which *I* knew was driving her crazy, as she needed to know what *everything* on campus meant!)

THE LAST ESSENE

Believe it or not, a time existed not all that long ago when there was no such thing as voicemail! If a call came to our office and no one picked up, it would be transferred to the person we would today call an administrative assistant. She (almost always a she) would then write a note and leave it in our mailbox.

The note which I was now being handed read as follows:

"Wayne-Daniel, found your mother. Bill"

This was followed by a phone number.

Miraculously, all fatigue and frustration left me! With profuse thank-you's, I ran into the building, vaulted the two floors to my office, and called Bill at the archive where he worked.

"Hi!" I said.

"Hi," he replied. "God *loves* you!!!"

"God loves you, too, Bill," I answered. "*What the hell happened?*"

My friend then went on to explain that he had gone into the vault at his work to find a document, when he just *happened* (?) to look down. There at his feet were two boxes, labelled, "Birth Records, Fall River, MA, 1951–52." I had been born in Fall River in 1952.

The boxes had been sent to this archive by mistake (*mistake?*) Bill had done his due diligence and had found my birth record, in that old-fashioned, reel-to-reel microfilm.

I don't remember the drive from my college to Bill's work. When I arrived, he showed me the microfilmed document with my birthmother's names, maiden and married. These had been crossed out, and my adoptive mother's name written over them. Across from this was my birthmother's husband's name likewise crossed out, the words "Father Unknown" written over it. This, too, had a line through it, and my adoptive father's name had been added.

I have often thought since how fortunate it was that this all happened before the widespread use of computers. Today, a simple click would have deleted all but my adoptive parents' names. As it was, the bright light streaming through the microfilm proclaimed with clarity "Who I was, who were my people, and where I had come from."

And I had Avel, now Bill, to thank for it. For the second time in my lives, he caused me not to be crossed out. My Process of Becoming was once again his Work of Mercy.

THE LAST ESSENE

He went on to use his expertise to help me find my birthmother's residence (The Jewish Home in Fall River. Mom liked Jews!) And most importantly, he welcomed my embrace of Whatever I Would Be, no matter where it led. The same could not be said of everyone.

The incredible blessing of past-life recognition is knowing that we are not left to navigate these journeys alone. Across the unfolding universe of lifetimes, we are companioned by souls who, whatever role they may play, and even without knowing it, still know *experientially* exactly how to be there for us.

Toda Raba, Amma, Ruth, Dothan, Avel! Thank you, all!

CHAPTER 8

Where Are We Really Going?

Sylvia then asked if I could fast-forward to the next thing of significance. I then saw what looked like an oasis, with water and palm trees. Behind and to the right was a sort of compound, with walls and square towers in the corners. Inside was a dirt courtyard and on the other side was a long house. Inside it there were rows of benches, amphitheater style. They were filled with men in tallits, gesturing, arguing, debating. This was an academy. My master (as I now thought of him) occupied a place in the center left; I stood right behind him. I was now 13–14 years old, and it was clear to me that I was his primary and special student, sort of an aide. I wore a tallit, too, but I was dressed all in white, the only one dressed that way. It was clear that the other men were very angry at my master for some reason; they were shouting and gesticulating toward him.

The scene then changed: we were in his quarters in the compound. There was a table, shelves, a mat over in the corner where I slept. On the table, Reb Ishmael had rolled out a scroll, and he was showing it to me and teaching me from it. I could see it was written in Greek characters. I asked him "Why do we have to study these pagans, who don't know God?" He replied that God gave a mind to everyone, and that we could learn "much from these people." I was skeptical. He then rolled up the scroll from each side, very carefully. "Yossi," he said, "what can you see now?" "Nothing, Master," I said. He just nodded and smiled at me as if to say, "Point made."

The scene then shifted back to the assembly room. The men were getting angrier and angrier at my master; they were all on their feet, waving their fists in the air and shouting. They were yelling, "Greek! Greek!" and "Heretic!" and "Impure!" I worried for him; as his disciple, I was allowed to be there, attending to him, even though I was still a boy. I was determined to protect him. Slowly he got up and began to walk down the levels toward the door. He seemed much older than when I'd first met him, whiter, with even more of a stoop, leaning more on his stick. As we walked away, I at his right shoulder, the crowd of men came closer, not blocking our way, but still kind of threatening. We just kept on walking; I looked them in the face, letting them know that I wouldn't let them harm my master. I remember one man with a very round face; he looked absolutely enraged and like he could be trouble, but I stared him down and he backed off a bit. I could tell that they weren't sure what to do with me; that they were somewhat afraid of the Essene, with stories of "powers," etc. We left the hall and walked out into the courtyard.

The scene shifted again. I was asleep in the night. I felt a poke on the front of my left shoulder; when I opened my eyes, I could barely make out the shape of my master. He'd poked me with his stick. He said, "Yossi, we're going." I said, "When?" He said, "Now." He didn't have an oil lamp; there was a little light coming through a window behind him. I got up. He handed me a rucksack; I felt inside and there were *some round loaves and what seemed to be dried dates or figs? He then handed me a water skin, which I slung over my right shoulder. Then we walked out the door, into the courtyard. It was dark, with a little moon, but we knew the grounds. We went out the tall, rectangular entrance way, and once more I was walking down a road to somewhere.*

We walked for what I knew to be about an hour. I saw that my master was crying. When I asked him why, he said, "We had to leave all the scrolls behind." I suggested that we'd gone far enough for now, and we lay down underneath a rock overhang by the side of the dirt road. I waited to make sure my master was asleep. I remember thinking to myself, "What good is all the wisdom, if they treat an old man like this?" Then I fell asleep.

Sylvia then asked if I could fast forward again. All I then saw was the two of us walking. Reb Ishmael was saying that we were going to another city "in the south, outside of Judea." But we might see Jerusalem first. I was excited as I'd never seen the city before, even though I knew it was in ruins.

At that point, our time was up, and Sylvia led me out of the meditation.

THE LAST ESSENE

Postscript

I asked Sylvia if it would be alright for me to begin doing some research on all this; earlier she had advised me not to, but just to allow the experience to sink in. She now thought it would be fine if I looked some things up.

When I got home, I went online. I did a Google search for "Josiah," but got lots of things about old Puritan New Englanders. I then typed in "Rabbi Josiah," and came to a site which spoke of a 2nd-century Talmudic master named Rabbi Josiah (Talmud is made up of commentaries on Torah and Jewish law, as well as legends and stories). Very little was known of him; he lived "in the south," and the Palestinian Mishnah was largely written in the north, in Galilee. It went on to say that he was the primary disciple of a Rabbi Ishmael ben Elisha! I clicked on that name and found information on him. One piece of scholarly speculation was that Ishmael ben Elisha was just a code name for another Rabbi, named Elisha ben Abuya, apparently an infamous heretic! He was condemned and expelled from the Sanhedrin; there were a number of possible explanations—that he was too devoted to Greek thought and tried to introduce it into the assembly, that he was a Gnostic, that he was a Christian. The article made a point of saying that all we know about Reb Elisha came from his enemies and wasn't very reliable. It is known that he was a major scholar with lots of contributions to Talmud, so much so, the speculation goes, that some rabbis didn't want to have to expunge all his teachings. So, they invented this code name to cover their flank. He is also referred to in the Talmud as "Akbar," "the Other."

WAYNE-DANIEL BERARD

Well, I was bowled over! I noticed that, unlike the other names I was seeing, this Rabbi Josiah was not listed as "ben anyone," no "son of." Just "Josiah," as if he had no parentage.

Christine and I are still reeling from this, and we're reflecting together on what it all means.

Commentary from Sylvia

After regression experiences, when the person has felt truly immersed in another place and time, they often express the wish to confirm certain historical facts, perhaps as a way of validating what has transpired as "real". Rarely is this seriously attempted. Once or twice, in my history of sessions, has someone done some research and come up with an exciting revelation such as: "such-and-such town really did exist or there really was a drought or a local war in that area during that era." Never before had one of my clients located and historically identified persons by name. I am as astonished as are Wayne-Daniel and Christine.

I had always been attracted to monasteries. I called them "small kingdoms of complete sense." When I was very young and contemplating formal Catholic religious life, I looked into monasticism as a possibility. My father, in his own inimitable way, "blew a gasket"—"You're at the top of your class!" he shouted.

"Why would you want to lock yourself up in some monastery? If you're going to be a priest, at least be one that helps people!"

To me, the attraction of the monastery was the totality of its experience and its commitment to building a community, no matter how small, that truly, unreservedly lived the beliefs its faith was espousing. Here was a place where everything was about God, just as I had always felt was the case all around me, but next to no one else seemed to feel it or see it.

Where can I run from Your love?
If I climb to the heavens, You are there;
If I fly to the sunrise or sail beyond the seas,
Still I'd find You there.

Psalm 139

I also wished desperately for an environment with as little distance as possible between what was said to be believed and how one actually lived. Not perfection—I knew that didn't exist. But a place and way of being where, even when one fell down, that falling itself was seen as part and parcel of the Process of Becoming, not as evidence that living one's belief was impossible, not as an invitation to comfortable mediocrity of spirit.

What I came to realize I was truly seeking can be summed up in a line from the poet Novalis:

Where are we really going? Always home.

In the end, the (very impatient) fourteen-year-old me opted for the semi-monasticism of Franciscan minor seminary (monasteries had a minimum age requirement). There I didn't find a semi-home or even semi-complete sense. But I had always remained deeply attracted to such places; I still make retreats, yarmulke on my head, at a Benedictine priory in the Green Mountains.

Now, in regression, I could see where this fascination with and call to the monastery came from. I had been ripped as child from the Essenic compound, very much a 1st-century Jewish monastery, and every bit a small kingdom of God's complete sense—or so it would have seemed to a boy not yet old enough to see the inevitable cracks and faults in every human environment. I would search for this home over and over again (I later learned) through multiple lives, unable to truly be happy anywhere, until realizing the source of my sense of homelessness as a trauma occurring in 70 CE. As with every effective therapy, that realization had led to healing.

Commentary from Sylvia

In the above section W-D has begun to reflect more deeply on the resonances of personality traits between his current life as W-D and that of Yossi: the call to the monastery life, his sense of homelessness. He has identified the trauma of Yossi's early life as one that has played out again in this life, and as he states, identifying the trauma is the first step in healing it. He goes on in the following sections to piece together elements of this current life's spiritual quests. In particular, W-D's ecumenical leanings and searching are understood as a continuation of what transpired in the life of Yossi.

And then there was the matter of ecumenism and interfaith.

I have been privileged to be a part of two great renewal movements, the Catholic Renewal of the 1960s and early '70s, and the Jewish Renewal Movement.

The Second Vatican Council of the Roman Catholic Church opened in October of 1962 and closed in December of 1965. The next year, 1966, I would enter seminary. It was an incredible time to be a young, progressively minded Catholic. The Sixties were a time of radical, thorough questioning of absolutely everything! Every cherished "truth" was now doubted, each time-honored tradition no longer honored just because of its survival in time. In seminary, we were writing our own Masses, rewriting the moral theology books—and perhaps most importantly for a reincarnated protégé of Elisha ben Abuya, the heretic, the Other—we were openly fraternizing with, indulging in, and finding the value of faiths other than our own. Vatican II had been designated an Ecumenical Council, after all—"Ecumenism" meaning to seek unity with other faiths. And we young seminarians were nothing if not seekers!

I especially dove directly into this interfaith wave! My parent would have died rather than set foot in a Protestant church, let alone (gasp!) a synagogue. I sought out these services, not to academically observe, but to actually pray with my brothers and sisters there. I went on retreat to a Vedanta Center, was a regular presence at Charismatic Renewal meetings, in which practices like praying in tongues, prophecy and its interpretation were regular occurrences. My Bible was Hermann Hesse's book *Siddhartha*, which had come to me in my seminary's summer reading list my freshman year; a copy of it has never left my book bag since. Later, my spiritual wanderings would take me even farther East, to meditation, yoga, and qi gong, and into the metaphysical realm, where I would realize my childhood ability, long repressed, to read auras and chakra energy. I would learn that I was a Shaman and a Summoner—one who could call up the souls of those who had passed and carry messages back and forth to those connected to them.

And, of course, I would become a commissioned interfaith clergyperson, a Peace Chaplain, and in that capacity serve as Director of Spiritual Life and Chaplain of my college.

And most important of all would be the discovery of my own Jewishness, my aforementioned Torah study with Alan Ullman, and my immersion in Jewish life, specifically as it is expressed in the Jewish Renewal Movement.

THE LAST ESSENE

Jewish Renewal, likewise begun in the 1960s, was founded by an Orthodox rabbi, Zalman Shacter-Shalomi, in reaction to what he found to be an over-institutionalized and unspiritual Jewish establishment. He called this movement "heart Judaism," and it emphasized a deep *and* ecstatic experience of the Divine and of community. Egalitarianism, openness to spiritual practices drawn from other traditions, singing and dancing in services, and most of all, a commitment to God, self, and others as *verbs*, as Processes of Becoming—these were and still are the marks of Jewish Renewal.

This, *this* was coming home, or the closest I had ever come to it. The Essenes were an odd mixture of ultra-orthodox Judaism and what one might call ancient New Age. They had set themselves apart because they felt it impossible to live a pure Jewish life in the world of their day, and yet they were known for their mysticism and esoteric abilities, sought after as healers, intuitives, and prophets. They were inveterate pacifists, forbidding even the sharpening of their own tools. And they believed that an apocalyptic battle between darkness and light was fast approaching, in the aftermath of which they would emerge to give rebirth to Jewish life and beyond.

My continual Process of Becoming in that life had led me from that community into the tutelage of Rabbi Ishmael, a cover-name for Rabbi Elisha ben Abuya, the leading spiritual Jewish radical-progressive of his day! From him, I would learn the futility a closed scroll, and through his experience (and my own) I would come to know the vitriol and violence of identity politics, the damage caused by the closed soul.

Almost nothing is known of my old teacher except that written by his enemies. To them he was a heretic, a polluter of Judaism, a threat. Through regression, I have been able to offer a first-hand account of this remarkable man, whose only crime was thinking and teaching that we can "learn much" from people different from ourselves. Is this why I was so attracted to Peace Chaplaincy, the motto of which is "to help us to love the ways that others love God"? Did something of my experiences of Rabbi Ishmael/Elisha form a response to interfaith openness and its opposite that seemed simply second nature to me in this life?

Walking that 1st-century road was not the only journey I would take with my great teacher; I soon came to recognize Rabbi Ullman as none other than this same Rabbi Ishmael! Yes, the brilliant but threatening teacher whose insights were nonetheless too valuable to be stricken from the Talmud continued his Process of Becoming into a life as the cutting-edge, inclusive Torah teacher of our day. As I write this, he is in Northern Ireland, leading joint studies for Catholics and Protestants. But then again, he Will Be Whatever He Will Be.

And what of Yossi, the Talmudic scholar Rabbi Josiah, son of no one? Having been given the green light by Sylvia to research, I found actual recorded teachings and opinions of his in Talmud.

THE LAST ESSENE

Imagine the sensation, the fulfillment, the full-circledness of Wayne-Daniel, the orphan, the Torah student, the interfaith chaplain and teacher, reading words that *he himself had written* over 1,800 years before, in a past life as an orphan, a survivor of violent intolerance, and a continual opener of diverse scrolls?

The process of self-discovery and the unfolding of historical narrative are, as Sylvia has said, prime parts of what makes these regressions so amazing. When the two are married together the result is nothing short of miraculous!

Session 5

Again, it took about ten minutes of sitting in stillness for anything to "happen." Finally, two dark shapes I could see began to clarify themselves; one was kind of squat and triangular, the other looked a bit like a big bell. When the "curtain parted," I could see that the triangular shape was a pyramid, and the bell shape was the head of the sphinx (although it looked less beaten up and its nose was there. I could clearly see the lines of the rows of big blocks of stone in the pyramid).

At first, I thought they were moving from my left to my right, but then realized that I was on a small boat with a sail. My master, Rabbi Ishmael, was with me. We were sailing back up-river; I had asked him if we could come down to see these monuments. Now we were heading back.

WAYNE-DANIEL BERARD

The boat eventually entered a canal on the left and came to a big lake; there was a spit of land in between the two, and we tied up there. From there we walked, my master seemed to have gotten quite a bit older and leaned on his stick more and more. I think I was about 19– 20. This was a big city which I knew to be Alexandria, Egypt. There were lots of different types of people from different places. The scene shifted to the school where my master was teaching, and we were living. Somehow, I knew it was in the Jewish Quarter of this city, but close to the Roman Quarter. The school had a walkway with a series of arches that we would walk beneath, and my master would teach and discuss as we walked along. Some of the students were Jews with beards, some were Greeks in chitons (no beards), some were Romans in short tunic-looking clothing. Others were Egyptians in what looked like long white nightshirts. They were shaved-headed. My master would speak in Greek, but I understood it in English. He was talking about "Torah being the Logos." He spoke as if the Torah were a living being and the scroll-form almost an incarnation or manifestation at the earthly level. There were two other primary men at the school, one was an Egyptian with a braided goatee growing from the center of his chin. The other was a Greek Jew, a bit older, shorter, with thinning hair. I didn't get any names. But I got the idea that the three of them sort of ran the place, although the Greek Jew seemed to have some additional leadership.

The scene shifted, and I was standing outside in a field. There was grass all around; I was standing in front of a rectangular hole in the ground; over to my left there was a wooden slab on the ground, and on top of that was something, about 4–4 1/2 feet long, all wrapped up in white cloth, very tight. All around stood other men, wrapped in tallits. I knew then that my master had died. `The men were praying and swaying; four other men (different, bare to the waist, looked like *laborers), picked up the slab by ropes that ran through a groove underneath its front and back; they lowered the slab into the hole by the ropes. Then we all walked off; there was a narrow canal and a wooden bridge. On the other side, a number of other men, older and younger, of different nationalities were gathered, waiting. I could tell they were quietly paying respects but didn't come to the graveside. As we walked back to the school, the Egyptian man was on my left and the Greek Jew on my right. The Egyptian asked me what I intended to do now. I told him that I wasn't sure, that I'd heard there were "others like me" living in a community far to the south but had never gone to investigate out of loyalty and respect for my master. Now I was considering doing so. The Greek Jew asked me if I would like to take my master's position at the school. He said that he knew I was young, but that I had been his disciple and knew his teachings well. It felt very good to be recognized, and I said I would accept, at least for a while.*

The extremely cosmopolitan, polyglot nature of ancient Alexandria is well known. It was apparently a city of contradictions. Founded by Alexander the Great himself in 331 BCE, it remained more Greek than Egyptian. It became known as a city of learning, attracting scholars from all over antiquity; The Great Library of Alexandria (actually, two libraries as two sites existed) sought nothing less than to amass all the knowledge in the entire known world. Nothing was out of bounds, no subject considered heretical or unworthy of attention.

At the same time, the city seemed deeply and sometimes explosively religious. The everyday people of Alexandria were not scholars, they were tradesmen, shop keepers, warehousemen, and dock workers who manned Alexandria's massive and frenetic port. Egypt, with its controlled overflow of the Nile River virtually guaranteeing a steady supply of rich silt to produce abundant crops, was the breadbasket of the Mediterranean and beyond, and all that wealth poured through the port of Alexandria. Where there was wealth there were immigrants and refugees; ancient Alexandria was probably the most diverse city on the planet, surpassing even Rome in that respect. Differing Gods, Goddesses, cults, and religious movements overflowed bounds as unstoppably as the Nile. For the most part, this presented little problem, as most did not engage in exclusivism of any sort. Indeed, the Zeus of the Greeks was identified with the Jupiter of the Romans and with the Amun-Ra of the Egyptians. The one exception was the Jews.

There had always been a major Jewish population in Egypt; it's little wonder that when the child Jesus was in danger from King Herod, his parents, clearly devout Jews, would flee to Egypt with him. They would be sure to find a large cultural enclave there. By the time Yossi and his teacher would have arrived in Alexandria, fully two of the city's five districts were thoroughly Jewish. But this major presence offered its own peculiar problems for this city of pluralism. By and large, the Jews of Egypt, especially those without an education, insisted on maintaining a cultural and religious distance from their counterparts. Their faith declared that only their One God was valid, and a complex system of Mosaic Law and its application virtually assured a spiritual Iron Curtain between the Jews of Egypt and the rest of the population.

THE LAST ESSENE

True, the Jewish scripture was translated into Greek (as this tongue would begin to replace Hebrew and Aramaic with each succeeding generation in Egypt), and more learned, "upper crust" Jews would seek to express Judaism in Greek philosophical terms, but there was also a push back against the "Hellenization" of Jewish life. This had culminated in 167–160 BCE in the successful revolt of the Maccabees family—staunch Hebrew nativists—against one of Alexander's former generals, and the establishment of the last independent Jewish state until the foundation of modern Israel in 1948.

In Yossi's day, both Egypt and Israel were Roman provinces, but the struggle between Hellenized and traditional Jews continued. In Alexandria in particular, that center of multiculturalism, clashes erupted regularly between most of the Jews living there (poorer, less educated and religiously conservative) and the predominantly Greek majority.

This had only grown stronger and more explosive in Yossi's young lifetime.

The destruction of the Essene compound, today called Qumran, was part of the general decimation of the Jewish state by Rome, occurring from 63 to 70 CE. During that time, Judea revolted against its Roman overlords; the revolution failed, the Great Temple in Jerusalem was destroyed, and a flood of refugees surged into Egypt and into Alexandria particularly. (Oddly enough, the destruction of the home of the pacifist Essenes has always been a mystery—why would the Romans bother with them at all? It was a question to which my past-life regression experience would finally provide an answer).

This influx of thousands if not more refugees from the Jewish homeland—much less cosmopolitan, far more conservative, and bent on preserving Jewish life from assimilation—would only add fuel to the pyre already near igniting in Alexandria and in Egypt as a whole. Into this atmosphere walk Elisha ben Abuya, already a conservative's boogie man, and his young protégé, Yossi the last Essene. They would become part of what was surely one of the most progressive academies in the city, one which apparently an Egyptian and a Greek Jewish intellectual ran together.

The similarity of this situation to that of own day in America is not lost on me. Vicious splits between philosophical and religious conservatives and liberals, the mass arrival of refugees from desperate circumstance and our reaction to them—the tenuous nature of our own experiment in pluralism—the present-life reality looms large over this past-life memory, and the events to follow in the life of Reb Yossi may offer lessons to more than myself personally.

CHAPTER 9

What Is Denied

Time went by (maybe a few months?). One morning, I leave the little house where I'd lived with the master, and the Egyptian is waiting outside the door. He tells me that there is a man, some sort of aide to the Roman governor. He is likewise a Roman, but he has a Jewish wife. They have a child. He has asked about tutoring, and the Egyptian wants to know if I will go speak with them. I agree.

Next thing I see, I'm walking out from the Jewish Quarter. I walk behind the school; there's a little square and a fountain. I cross an arched wooden bridge over a canal; there are docks there, and men unloading barrels and sacks. As I walk along, the neighborhood becomes very residential; nice, larger homes with columns in front. I remember that the Egyptian said I'd recognize the house as it had eight columns. And there it was, on the right. I go under the portico supported by the columns, and the shade feels very good. There's a servant standing there; he's very dark with no shirt. I tell him who I am, and he leads me inside. In a room the Roman is standing beside an empty chair; he is wearing a white robe that folds over one shoulder with a blue stripe. His wife sits on a big pile of cushion on the floor to his left (the chair is unusual looking; it's made out of slats of wood bent into two hour-glass shapes, joined at the center. You'd sit in the top "half" of the hourglass, and the bottom-half would support you). Anyway, the man does all the talking. His name is Cornelius. I never get the woman's name. He says that his wife is "involved with the Christos." He asks me about him and his group. Are they seditious? I tell him that I know very little about them, but that I will investigate and report to him. Someone enters from the right; it's a young girl, about 14–15. She's got an incredibly beautiful face! Big, innocent brown eyes; dark hair (women here don't seem to wear headcovers). She sits on cushions next to her mother and looks up at me. Her father introduces her as his daughter, La'nah. I'm having terrible trouble not staring at her; I keep looking straight ahead. I say that I'd been told I was there about tutoring. He says that he'd like me to tutor his wife and daughter, to "keep them on the path." I get the idea that this is some sort of euphemism for staying on center, not getting too extreme in their views. I agree; I'm very excited by the prospect of seeing the girl again. The man asks my fee, and I tell him that there isn't any, that it isn't my practice to take money for imparting knowledge, and that all my needs are met by the school. But he insists that it wouldn't do for him to be beholden and says he will pay me something. I bow a little to him, then to the two women; I'm so glad to be able to look at the girl. Then I leave; the servant leads me out.

I don't know what to do with my feelings; my heart is racing (and, sitting in the chair, it is, too!). She is so amazingly beautiful, and not just to look at. I get such a strong feeling of openness and warmth from her. I'm really taken with her; I'm breathing heavy in the hot air. All I can think of is her. But I have no one to talk to about any of this; no one older I can turn to.

THE LAST ESSENE

So, love has finally come to Yossi the Essene. And he, it would seem, was no more prepared for it than was his reincarnation, Wayne-Daniel the ex-seminarian.

So many tumblers clicked as I experienced this part of my regression. Yossi had been raised from birth among the celibate Essenes; he had never even seen a woman before his encounter with Amma, so much so that he didn't even recognize her as one initially. I entered Franciscan seminary at fourteen and had made the decision to do so by the time I was twelve. Women were likewise kept from the grounds of our seminary, except for family on "visiting Sundays" and the odd female employee—a librarian, a teacher a secretary to the Rector—always older women with little chance of being a "near occasion of sin" in the actions or thoughts of we seminarians. This was accompanied by an underlying disdain for women; the seminary, like the Essene compound, was an extremely masculine environment, one in which it was made clear that the feminine was not only unwelcome but dangerous to our way of life and our vocations.

One example springs to mind: From its founding in 1904 to the appointment of a new, more liberal Rector in 1968, the seminary was completely cloistered. Seminarians were not allowed off the grounds except under very controlled circumstances; sixty-four-years-worth of young priests-in-training had come and gone and never set foot in the small town situated at the bottom of the hill upon which the school sat. In order to mail letters (we were required to write home regularly), one had to place the letter, unsealed, in a box at the door to the Office of the Prefect of Discipline. I was understood that he read all mail, in-coming and outgoing—or at least could do so. Any mail coming to us always had its envelope slit open.

At the close of noon meal each day, The Prefect, who sat on a riser at the front of the refectory, would read a list of names of those he wanted to see in his office, the "In Trouble List." One particular day, we were all surprised to hear one specific name read out—one of my classmates who was the mildest-mannered, least troublesome kid one could imagine. He himself was flabbergasted and very anxious about being called to the office—would I come with him? Of course, I said yes.

We climbed the steps to the Prefect's office in the towered main building of the school (which greatly resembles Hogwarts—but without the magic. These stairs, like everything else in seminary, were committed to never moving!) I had to wait outside the door. After what seemed like a very long time, my friend emerged, completely red-faced and filled with what seemed a combination of disgust and rage. Once we were a safe distance from the building, he told me what had happened: As he'd stood in front of the desk, the Prefect had tossed a stack of pastel-colored envelopes across it and gruffly said, "Tell her not to write anymore." My friend was completely flummoxed; he looked at the letters, then made the realization. "They're from my sister," he said.

The priest replied, "You don't have a sister," and accused my friend of carrying on an illicit relationship with a female! After all, the letters were signed, "Love," and talked about how much the writer cared about and missed my friend.

My friend went in to explain that he had been a "late in life" baby, that he had a much older sister, grown and gone, who had not been at his house for the "home visit" by the Vocation Director. The school simply didn't know she existed and had jumped to the wrong conclusion about the letters.

The Prefect muttered something along the lines of, "We'll see about that," and phoned my friend's home. His mom assured him that she did indeed have an older daughter, whose name and address matched those in the letter and on the envelope. Without even an apology, Father Prefect waved my friend out of the office.

Such was the attitude toward women, love, and matters of the heart in general. I feel strongly it would have been the same in any institutional culture that mandated celibacy, whether it was the 1st-century Essenes of the 20th-century Franciscans. What is denied is despised.

What amazed me was the repetition across lifetimes of my being drawn to such places, complete with the need (literally, time and again) for the agonizing process of ripping myself free from their attitudes and pathology.

WAYNE-DANIEL BERARD

Commentary from Sylvia

People engaged in any kind of retrospective self-analysis often are amazed at the dynamic called repetition compulsion—how we repeat the same pattern over and over. The past life perspective extends the frame of the source of such a dynamic, allowing us to understand even more fully where the original conflicts occur. In more traditional therapies it is assumed that childhood dilemmas are at the core of repetition compulsions. What I have found is that sometimes a past life story with the traumas and features of that life can offer the necessary key to unlocking the answer to "where did this all begin?"

And how could such an inherent contradiction manage to exist, let alone flourish in the first place? We are speaking of matters centered on God, on the heart, on relationships of the spirit between the Divine and human, and among humans for one another. How could any of that possibly morph into a reality that, in the name of the Great Compassion, renders its most committed followers contemptuous of or simply unable to love?

The opportunity that regression had given me to compare—to relive! These two communities side by side in memory had left me with at least the beginnings of an understanding of them—and of the person they had created me to be.

For a moment, imagine drawing a square on a piece of paper. The four lines making up the square are the bound of one's faith tradition, that piece of existential real estate that encompasses our spiritual identity. All the beliefs, traditions, teachings, the longings of the soul and heartfelt experiences of religion are represented by those equilateral marks. In terms of spirituality, this is home. This is what drew you to the square in the first place.

But imagine further that, *within* that square, there is no place for *any* of that.

Within the square, the heart is banished; depth of feeling or the expression of them is held in scorn. What matters here, what is taught and encouraged, is logic—cool, unaffected reason. The educational system within the square is most demanding and classical in nature: Greek, Latin, and a modern language, four years of math, four years of everything. Theology is emphasized, but it is the cold, extremely systematic discipline of Thomas Aquinas and the Scholastics. No one speaks about a lived spirituality, the way of the heart, the journey of the soul. Spiritual practice is relegated to the very formal daily Mass, morning and evening prayer.

And even this highly intellectual, Rationalistic milieu cannot threaten the boundaries of the box,

Cannot bulge the walls or (*Deus absit!*) open a door in them. God forbid! As Aquinas himself said, consummate Rationalist though he was, if your reason disagreed with your Faith (as expounded by the Church), your reason must be faulty. Follow your Faith. Obey the Church.

For this very masculine, very left-brained spiritual culture, the worst enemy was the emotions, the heart—you know, all the "trappings of the feminine." The Church which had sought to step into the shoes of a collapsing Roman Empire, believing it had forgotten its *gravitas*, *dignitas*, and *auctoritas* in favor of self-indulgence and undisciplinedness, had much in common with the Essenes who, mystics though they might have been, demanded meticulous attention to the Law of Moses, the keeping of the sabbath, and to ritual cleanness. They went so far as to retreat into their own closed community in the desert to stay pure from any diluting influences, including women. In both cases, all this was done in the name of a God who definitionally defied logic, knew no boundaries, and "whose *love* is faithful forever."

But you might ask, what of the great renewal movement of Vatican II, described earlier—the questioning of everything, the liberalization of the Church? Didn't this redraw the four lines of the square, make them more porous, more malleable? Wouldn't spiritual renewal have to include a reintroduction of the heart to the head, of the long-neglected feminine to the all-too masculine?

The answer, at least long term, was unfortunately, no.

Commentary from Sylvia

I wonder here: isn't there always a tension between faith and reason in religious traditions? Also, between personal experience /open expression and adherence to rules and rituals that can feel constricting? These seem to be universal themes reflected in one person's story.

Remember, I had entered seminary only a year after the close of the Council. The spirit of change, of openness and of relating from the heart had barely begun in the Church, and it would take a long time for it to trickle down from the Vatican, through the parish system, Catholic colleges and universities, and finally to seminaries. And "trickle down" is exactly the right term, because the Vatican II Renewal was a top-down affair. An elderly Pope, John XXIII, chosen as a safe compromise candidate, shocked the world by initiating the changes of the Council—as well he could. The Pope was an absolute monarch. The people of the Church were certainly not consulted and were as blindsided by the changes as my friend had been by Father Prefect and the letters. The one thing that did not change, the one thing that might have guaranteed continued openness *to* change, was control. That most masculine of traits remained firmly intact, and just as firmly in the hands of celibate males—there would be no married priests in the Latin Rite, no women priests at all.

This would explain how a seminary in which its students were experimenting with rewriting the sacred Mass would still read their mail, in-coming and out-going. This could help make sense of the fact that, although we seminarians were eventually allowed off-grounds in the afternoons, the girls we might get to know there were still not allowed on the grounds, ever.

In this universe, control made change possible. Everything could change but that. And so, any opportunity for love to truly enter that square found itself impaled upon the sharp corners of its masculinity. Pope John died less than a year after the closing of his Council. His successor unilaterally banned the birth control pill for Catholic women. *Plus ca change . . .*

What consequences might the world of the Essenes *and* of Catholic seminary have upon the young psyche of a boy immersed in both? What effects would this have on the ability to give-in to the divine wonder of human love, to step outside the square and even—unthinkable! —see God in the feminine?

To Yossi reaching for breath after a few short minutes in the presence of La'nah, who would one day be the Lovely Christine of all too similar affect, it must have seemed he was going mad.

But then, as the great poet and dramatist Colderon de la Barca noted:

"When Love is not madness, it is not Love."

CHAPTER 10

Only Love Is Real

Commentary from Sylvia

The following scenes quickly pulled me into a near trance as I found myself witness to a fascinating time in history, the years of early Christianity, shown via details of everyday life and conversation. The vivid scenery, objects, clothing, and the content of the conversations, all combined in a story that was compelling in and of itself and offered a glimpse into the world where these historical forces were operating. For long stretches, it was like watching a film.

At the time of the regression sessions, I had no idea of the parallels in Wayne-Daniel's current life. And it would be years, not until reading this text, before I would learn the profound resonances that he discovered and explored for himself and in his primary therapy. What was apparent at the time was that there were at least two main threads which stood out in this work: the insights into religious and cultural evolution, and the insights into the nuances of personal past-life influences.

WAYNE-DANIEL BERARD

The rest of the story unfolding here speaks for itself. WD intersperses the narrative with a deep personal analysis which had been aided by his psychotherapy, a process where he obviously debriefed and worked through the regression material.

That night I toss and turn; I can't sleep. The next morning, which is Saturday, I walk deeper into the Jewish Quarter. There are stalls, an open-air market, but no vendors; it's Shabbat. Still, there are people walking about. I come to a beit midrash on the right; it's white-washed with a dome. I go in; I can tell that services have just ended. There's a young man in a tallit, he's about my age, sitting on one of the benches inside; he comes forward and hugs me. He's my friend; his name is Yoachanan. He's a bit of a dandy; he has very light brown hair and beard, very fastidiously trimmed. He also perfumes himself; I can smell it when he hugs me (and I can smell that smell as I sit in the chair). We sit and talk; he likes to kid and tease me. He asks me when I'm going to come to service; I ask him when he's going to come to the school. I'd like him to teach there. I ask what he knows about the Christos and his followers. He says they are "harmless, like children." That they talk about everybody loving everybody, "very unrealistic, but harmless." I ask if they are heretics. He laughs and says, "With a master like yours was, and teaching in that school, you ask about heretics?" I don't like that so much. He then says that "they can't agree among themselves about the Christos." Some see him as the Logos, others as just a great teacher. I don't tell him anything about La'nah; he'd just tease me.

The scene shifts, and I'm back at the Roman's house, teaching. We're in an enclosed garden in the back, very nice. There's a carved face in the back wall, and water comes out its mouth into a rectangular stone basin. We sit on wooden benches; there's a table behind us with scrolls laid out.

The girl is just filling me up. I try to address them both, but I have the worst time not looking at her all the time. When I leave the house this time; I'm all the way to the fountain before I realize where I am. I don't even remember the walk. All I can think of is her. But I'm very torn. What about being Assah? What about keeping that "way?" Assah don't marry or have much to do with women. And what about that community in the south? What if there really are others like me? But am I actually like that still? What about La'nah? I think of her as being "just a child." But, God, she's all I can think about. Everything has been so empty inside before this.

I've suggested to the mother that we meet twice a week (same price!). She agrees. I really just want to see La'nah more often. One day, when I go there, the servant meets me like usual, but tells me that his mistress is sick. I have the worst time understanding him, even in this "past-life vision." His accent is very strange. Finally, I see that he's trying to say that his mistress "is sick with the sickness of women." I'll still meet with the daughter. He'll "stand there," he says. So, I'm going to be alone (almost) with La'nah!!!

We're in the garden; we've been studying the wisdom of Solomon, on parents and children. The servant is standing over against the wall at the entrance to the garden, behind us. At one point, La'nah asks if we can't study something different in Solomon. I ask her what, and she gestures to a scroll already opened on the table. I stand and go to it and read aloud, "Come now, my love. My lovely one, come." I can't talk anymore; I can hardly breathe. My heart's in my throat. I turn back to La'nah, and she's crying; tears are running down her cheeks.

Then she covers her face with her hands, gets up and runs out of the garden. I just stand there for a second; the servant is just looking straight ahead, very impassively. Then I leave; he walks me out but says nothing.

I'm an absolute mess! She loves me! And I love her! Oh SHIT!!! What do I do? Who can I talk to? I can hardly breathe. I have to stop, to catch my breath. This seems like a panic attack. I'm so glad, and scared, and confused, and torn. I have no idea where to turn.

This is the point where Sylvia asks me to "put these feelings away, assign them to the

'tape' of that life," and she calls me out of the meditation.

I have no doubt whatsoever that the girl is Christine. She even looks a lot like her, although much younger, and her head and face are shorter. There's still a sort of "baby pudge" to it, but in a very womanly way (think young Jennifer Connolly). She is just gorgeous, magnetic.

I want to add that, on the ride home, Christine said that it "would be okay if it wasn't" her. That I needn't be afraid to say that. But, boy, that is not the case. This is she, all the way! Absolutely.

This was the most difficult, emotionally, of all the sessions, much worse than when the original compound was burning. I was absolutely wracked about my feeling for the girl; I could feel the anxiety, the panic, the shortness of breath and heart pounding. I even experienced an ache in the upper front of my left shoulder, which happens when I'm under extreme, prolonged stress. It took me quite a while to "come back." I could tell that Sylvia was a little concerned; she spent more

THE LAST ESSENE

time than usual working me toward "getting back into this present body."

WHEW!!!

In his beautiful book *Only Love Is Real* Brian Weiss offers these words,

There is someone special for everyone. Often there are two or three or even four. They come from different generations. They travel across oceans of time and the depths of heavenly dimensions to be with you again. They come from the other side, from heaven. They look different, but your heart knows them. Your heart has held them in arms like yours in the moon-filled deserts of Egypt and the ancient plains of Mongolia. You have ridden together in the armies of forgotten warrior-generals, and you have lived together in the sand-covered caves of the Ancient Ones. You are bonded together throughout eternity, and you will never be alone.

Your head may interfere: "I do not know you." Your heart knows.

He takes your hand for the first time, and the memory of his touch transcends time and sends a jolt through every atom of your being. She looks into your eyes, and you see a soul companion across centuries. Your stomach turns upside down. Your arms are gooseflesh. Everything outside this moment loses its importance.

Such was the moment I was reliving from the 2nd century, as I sat in a chair in the 21st. Right in that office, my stomach turned upside down, my arms were gooseflesh. A jolt has indeed passed through every atom of my body—twice!

It was *so real*—real as only an actual and definitional memory can be.

Not that I had any doubts, but in Christine I had found my great love. Again.

Several years earlier, I had written her this poem:

Christine Day

today

we declare our

independence from

the rest of

everything

        —let it all

        tread on

        itself—

THE LAST ESSENE

today is

measured

in thankyous,

sixty thank

yous to the

hour, twenty

four to the course

of thankyou across

a cloudless thank

you.

Christine let there

be, and it was

Christine and all

saw that it was

shabbat

stopping

in you resting

everyday,

the messiah's eve

everyday death's

WAYNE-DANIEL BERARD

>angel wavers, oh
>
>it's you and passes
>
>gladly everyday
>
>becomes another
>
>night and day,
>
>Christine Day.

And now I was remembering vividly another Christine Day, or rather a La'nah Day.

The parallels were uncanny.

The Lovely Christine is my second wife. She had been my student in an adult-ed class at her Catholic parish on "The Jewishness of Jesus and of Christianity." We immediately became great friends. I walked her through her divorce, and she walked me through mine. As in the 2nd century, Christine realized and expressed ahead of me a deepening of feelings. I even recall sitting across from her at a little café and bookshop (Jewish—how apropos!) We were laughing at something; I reached out and touched her hand. She immediately "jolted" back. What was wrong, I asked? Christine didn't reply. But later that week, she was driving and listening to a tape of Dr. Weis' *Many Lives, Many Masters*. When it spoke about recognizing past-life love in the electric moment of a touch, she knew that this was exactly what had happened to her in that coffee shop. Of course, when she called me and told me so, my reply was, "Oh, you don't fight fair!"

You see, I was (once again) resistant of Great Love.

I had just gotten divorced. I told myself I was not ready, that the feelings I was experiencing might just be an attempt to fill in the holes that had erupted in my life. Truth be told (and I had told it to Christine) there had been someone else in my heart earlier in the process of my marriage's dissolution; that had not worked out, but the emotional residue still seemed to coat my feelings.

No matter, Christine assured me. She was certain we had been together before and would be again. She could wait.

What my regression experience was teaching me was the massive power of early-life conditioning, even across the lifetimes. As a young, spiritually oriented Catholic boy, I had been "marinated," shall we say, in the attitudes and approach to life of that very male-dominated culture, one that was dismissive if not outright hostile to the feminine and everything it saw as associated with it— relationship, heartedness, even love itself. My experience in the 20th-century version of the Essene compound had only strengthened this exponentially. In place of the heart came an overinflated centering on the head—on absolute intellectual assent to the doctrines and strict parameters of one's faith, and on a commitment to a life solely led by reason, within the boundaries of those parameters. In short, I had been conditioned toward *always* maintaining *control* under the aegis of ever "being reasonable," of clearly, and most of all dispassionately, weighing every option, every move solely in the cold light of reason. There was nothing "unspiritual" about this, I thought. Didn't Dante's own Virgil say to him, upon entering the Inferno, "Here you will see the wretched people who have lost the good of Intellect"?

Leaving those boyhood places, whether Essenic or Franciscan, even after they no longer existed (my seminary had closed two years after my graduation), I had not left those ingrained and carried-over attitudes behind. I could see now that even in my first marriage, I had held love somewhat at a distance. The heart was all well and good, but I was always terrified that, given much running room, it would overrun the head.

I did not realize how much of me was still an Essene, still a seminarian. Yossi had promised himself to preserve his old way of life, even after the Essenes had been destroyed; he even still toyed with the idea of seeking out a "community to the south" that sounded similar to his old home. I had at one time considered seminary in another Christian denomination with which I'd became involved. Yet, here was Yossi, about to become a teacher in the most un-Essenic academy imaginable, and he was still panic-stricken at the affect love might have on a way of life that had long ago ceased to be who he truly was. And I, who had embraced my Renewal Jewishness and become an interfaith clergy-person, had still had great difficulty releasing my grip on my defense mechanism, which Alexander Pope called "the God in the Mind" (Reason), in favor of the twenty-four unending hours of thank-yous that was Christine Day.

THE LAST ESSENE

Dr. Weiss goes on to say in *Only Love Is Real*,

He may not recognize you, even though you have finally met again, even though you know him. You can feel the bond. You can see the potential, the future. But he does not. His fears, his intellect, his problems keep a veil over his heart's eyes.

Would Yossi allow his Great Love to sweep that veil aside? Had I, truly, allowed mine?

Sylvia was not alone in her concerns.

CHAPTER 11

Thinking Past the Heart

Session 6

Sylvia and I spent a good amount of time speaking about the emotional process of these sessions, about how I was doing with the "coming out of it" at the end of each session, if I was having any insights regarding the significance of the people and events in the sessions. I related to her how the correspondence of many of the people in the past life to those in my present life had become clear only after I'd recognized Christine in La'nah.

We then began the session. I found that I went in much more quickly than the last time. Sylvia suggested to my "Higher Self" that it focus back on the tutoring with La'nah and her mother. But instead, the shapes that began to concretize looked like a pyramid and a sort of lop-sided mound. I said to myself, "Pyramids? I've already seen this." But as the scene became clearer, I could see that this was a new place. The mound was a sand dune, crested like a wave, and the pyramid was one of several; they were smaller and, in some cases, nearly

THE LAST ESSENE

swamped with sand. This spot was outside the city, and I would come here to walk and be alone, to think. It was apparently abandoned, like an old graveyard, and the desert was reclaiming it. I could feel the soft, very warm sand on my sandaled feet. I was thinking about La'nah, about how much I loved her, about the Assah, my feelings of loyalty to that way of life—generally feeling torn and overwhelmed by the whole thing.

I walked back toward the city, over a rather big arched, stone bridge, and into the Jewish Quarter. I came into the school compound and headed toward my quarters, which were on the left/middle of the square. I could see someone standing by my door; it was the Egyptian Master. He was taller than me, perhaps in his late 60s; he wore an Egyptian headpiece (like a striped bandana with starched panels that came down to his shoulders) and he had a goatee, just in the middle of his chin, sort of long and braided. We bowed to each other, and he asked me to walk with him. We crossed the yard toward his quarters. He asked me if I was alright. I said of course. I hadn't seemed myself, he said. I felt pretty stupid; I thought I'd done a good job of keeping my inner turmoil to myself. I said that, no, no, I was fine. We got to his "apartment" in the upper right corner of the square; he asked me in. Being one of the leaders of the place had its perks, apparently. His place is basically two units on a corner; it has a southern exposure and gets lots of light. There was Egyptian-looking furniture, rugs, etc. He walked over toward a back window; underneath it was a narrow table, on it was a rectangular piece of gray granite, about 2 ½ feet long, eight inches wide, six inches deep. On it were placed a small clay pyramid in the center; to its left was a sculpted and painted head of a dog or a wolf; to its right, a bird with a head piece. The man said, "I'm going to tell you something I've never told anyone. But you must swear by your God that you'll never tell anyone else." I swear. Then he *takes the objects off the stone and turns it over twice, so that its bottom is now on top. The bottom is carved; you can see that this was part of a column and belonged set on its end. In the upper right is carved a big disc, like a sun; there are rays coming down from it and each ray ends in a little hand with its index finger pointing. Down in the lower left are the figures of a man and a woman; they're more like caricatures, long and slim. They're kneeling back on their heels and looking up at the disc.*

The man asks me if I know what this is. I say I don't (the funny thing is that my conscious self knows that it does recognize the images but can't "bring up" the information). The Egyptian then goes on to say that the disc represents the God Ahten, that over a thousand years before, a pharaoh had promoted the idea of one God, of whom all the other Gods were just manifestations. He built temples, cities, etc., to this God, but when he died, the new pharaoh yielded to the priests of those old Gods and had the memory of Ahten obliterated, all the public image effaced, his temples abandoned.

He then asks me if I know his name. I don't; everyone calls him the Egyptian master. I'm not on his social level and wouldn't call him by name anyway. He tells me it is "Pote," that his family was originally made up of priests of this Ahten and still worship him in secret. His real name is "Ahtenpote." He says that, even today, there are people who would kill him if it was known he still followed this God. He says, "See, Yossi, we're very much alike. We both pray to the sun." I tell him that, although Assah face the sun in the morning and pray, we don't really worship the sun. He says that he knows; it's a symbol for God, just like it is for him. He then says that he knows that I leave the compound before dawn every morning for this prayer and asks if he can go with me and we could pray together? I say of course; I'd be honored. He then says, "Now, Yossi, I've told you my secret; won't you tell me yours?" He says he knows something is bothering me, and that, now that I know his secret, I have "leverage," in case he would ever betray mine, so I needn't worry about that. I sink back in the chair that's behind me; my insides are all heaving. I begin to tell him everything—about La'nah, about my feelings, the words from Solomon, then I go back to the beginning: the fire, the desert, the goats, Amah, Dothan, Ruth, the academy and the escape, everything. I'm crying (in the chair as well). It's all so overwhelming. I don't know what to do about La'nah. I feel like my feelings are betraying my past, that I need to keep the Assah alive. What about Avel and everybody else? Besides, I don't know "how to be out there." I don't know how to have a girlfriend or a wife; I've never had possessions or a family. I've always lived in institutions, like "The Place," or academies and schools. I don't have any money; I can't pay a "bride price." "I'm so lost," I say.

Pote reaches over and puts his hand on my left wrist; no one ever touches around here (or, really, ever in this life that I can recall). He says, "Yossi, what is the sun for?" I can't believe this; he's asking me riddles now?!! I need help, advice. But I answer, "For light." "And what else?" he asks. "For heat," I say. "Yes," he says, "for light and for warmth. You need both. The sun always gives both. Don't take the light without the warmth, Yossi," he says. "You love this girl?" he asks. I answer that I do, with all my heart. He says that he's already discussed the matter with the other Master, the Greek Jew, and they've agreed to pay the bride price for me, "for your old Master, who was very dear to us." He says, "I have no sons of my own." I look up at him; how did he know about La'nah and me? He says, "I'm too old not to recognize love sickness when I see it." Besides, he says, he knows the servant at the house and sees him in the Egyptian Quarter. "My little mistress is in love," he'd joke with him. "What have you brought into our house, old man?"

I thank him. I tell him it's just so much at once, that I need to think. He gets down on one knee and squeezes my wrist a little. He says, "Think, of course, think. But don't think too long, Yossi." Then he says emphatically, "Don't think past your heart." But I can tell that I'm not getting the full meaning of the words he's using (when people talk in these regressions, I do hear their voices running along in their language, but in my head, I hear the words in English. But sometimes it's as if the babel-fish in my head needs to fine-tune itself. Some of the words seem to be idioms or to have multiple shades of meaning). Then I hear him say, "Don't think away your heart, Yossi."

He then asks me if I know why the Romans destroyed the place where I'd lived. I say no, that we were peaceful and would only respond to defend ourselves and then only the minimal we had to do. He says that "the leadership that survived" had told the Romans that we were dangerous and a threat; they wanted to eliminate any groups that could compete with them. "You were betrayed, Yossi, by the leaders" (the word he uses means more like 'holy leaders'), "just as I and mine were." He then says again that he'd like to join me for dawn prayer, the next morning.

At this point Sylvia brought me out of the regression. I tried a new visualization: seeing a photo album and closing the cover of it, putting it in a wooden box (like a big jewelry box). Then I saw our side yard with the beech tree; I saw myself placing the box under the tree, then coming around the back, through the gate, back into the house. The dogs are barking; I visualize myself checking the phone messages and emails, just like I do when I come in from being out somewhere. This seems to help my transition out of the regression a great deal.

There is a well-known saying, "When the student is ready, the Master appears"—well-known, and in my lives, past and present, quite true!

In his hour of spiritual and emotional crisis, Yossi found the guidance he needed in the person of Pote the older Egyptian Master and co-founder of the Academy (which regression would show was simply known as The Bridge School, for its proximity to a bridge between a Jewish and Roman quarter of Alexandria).

In my present life, just such a Master had also appeared, at a time not so much of active crisis for me as of spiritual "stuckness." He was likewise an older man, my father's age, in fact. He was a Catholic Permanent Deacon (as distinguished from a Deacon on the way to Priesthood), an ardent letter-writer and a poet. His name was Philip Anderson, and like his counterpart eighteen centuries earlier, he was a teacher of the Way of the Heart.

Hardly a surprise, I now saw, as Pote and Phil had been the same person.

Pote would show the young Essene two truths critical to his future. First, he would move him past the dichotomy, the "either-or-ness" which had formed his approach to everything in his life, God, people, meaning—and love! The sun gives both light *and* warmth, Pote would urge him to understand. "Don't take the light without the warmth." Reason had long been identified with Light, and rightly so. But the sun likewise gave warmth—emotion, comfort, tenderness, and love! The mind and heart could no more be separated than the sun could be split between light and warmth. To expel one in an effort to safeguard the other was impossible, an illusion. An embrace of the *balance* was what was required, and Yossi's life to date had been so lopsided, so resistantly out of balance that only an unexpected *explosion* of romantic love—and plenty of it! —could hope to right the scales.

As my regressions would come to show, it was not only in matters of romance that Yossi was a stranger. For all his strict preservation of the Essenic way, the very idea of God's love as a felt reality or of Yossi's possible love for God had never even surfaced in his consciousness. Having any sort of personal relationship with the Divine was as foreign a concept as having a personal relationship with a woman. Clearly, for Yossi and La'nah, his way to I Will Be Whatever I Will Be lay through "I Will Be My Love For Her."

When I first met Phil Anderson, I was what I would describe as a "treadmill Catholic activist." I was a liturgical musician, high-school religion teacher, Bible study, prayer group, and retreat leader; I was constantly, almost compulsively, "doing things for God." And yet I felt no closer to God than I ever had—in fact, just the opposite. Spiritually speaking, I was stuck.

Phil and I were serving on the same retreat team for high-school seniors. Having young children of my own at home, I commuted back and forth to the retreat center, rather than staying over. I had just returned to the center one late morning when I met Phil out for a walk; it was rec time. As I joined him, I apologized for having missed his talk on prayer; he proceeded to give it to me! As we walked along together, he spoke of a prayer not of formal words, not of petition or thanksgiving or even praise, neither was it the "conversational prayer" that I had engaged in all my life. Rather, this was a prayer of listening, a prayer of stillness. It lived in that phrase from the Psalms, "Be still and know that I am God." In this form of prayer, one just sat in stillness, centered on one's breath (which Genesis 2 describes as God's very life within us). The mind, the intellect was not rejected, not disparaged; it was more like a dove tucking its head beneath its wing. The mind was stilled, the heart was opened. As Lao Tzu commented 2,500 years ago:

> The Master doesn't seek
>
> fulfilment.
>
> Not seeking, not expecting,
>
> she is present, and can
>
> welcome all things.

Well, every light in my insides went off! (My regression would show me how similar this was to my first sight of La'nah—truly the heart is One!) I asked Phil how I could learn more about this "Centering Prayer"; he told me that he had built a small structure in his yard just for this purpose ("6 feet by 6 feet, just under the tax limit!") Phil had five children at home and quiet could be at a premium. He called this place The Hermitage, and had dedicated it to his great spiritual influence, St. Therese of Lisieux, known as The Little Flower. He would pray and meditate there and invited me to join him.

I don't think the poor man knew what he'd let himself in for!

The experience of this prayer of listening and stillness was like water in the desert for me. Every Saturday morning for at least a year I trekked the forty-five minutes from my home to Phil's Hermitage, where we sat on the floor of this tiny space and opened our hearts to the wordless immensity of the Divine. And yet there were books! Phil gifted me with Basil' Pennington's *Centering Prayer*, the anonymous *Way of a Pilgrim*, Catherine de Hueck Doherty's *Poustinia* (Russian for "hermitage"), and Carlo Carretto's *Letters from the Desert*, among many others. We went on quiet retreats together, and even travelled to Europe, where Phil would realize his lifelong dream of praying where his beloved Therese had prayed.

From these Christian forms of meditation, I would travel farther East, studying Zen and engaging in mantra-centered meditation, immersing myself in the spirit of Buddhism, Taoism, mystical Judaism., and the Metaphysical.

THE LAST ESSENE

What a joy to realize that, in the 20th century, I had brought together those who, in different ways, had saved my life in the 1st and 2nd, Avel and Pote, as my dear friend Bill soon became a regular in Phil's Poustinia.

Most amazing is what Phil modeled for me in terms of "yes, and" rather than "either/or." In his prayer and meditation practice, Phil was luminously (and proudly) both Eastern and Western. Though lovingly devoted to his Catholic tradition, his Hermitage was his own interfaith spiritual Academy, where he could continue the work he had engaged in eighteen centuries earlier as Pote, the Egyptian Master. I would likewise describe him with the Gospel's words, as someone who could "bring out of his storehouse both the old and the new" (Mt 13:52). A much older, Western man, Phil could meditate in the style of a contemporary Indian yogi *and* of a 19th-century Carmelite nun. As he had in his life as Pote, he did not need to discard one form of divine light in order to regard another. He was open and could welcome all things.

And all things included me. Philip Anderson was much more than a once and present Spiritual Teacher in my life. As the Egyptian Master and the Permanent Deacon, he loved me; he listened to me, put up with me, took care of me, and delighted in me, as I did in him. And he companioned me, in the deconstruction of imbalance between heart and mind. Even now, centuries and decades after the end of their particular incarnations, I still hear our heart-conversations enlightening me, as in one of Phil's haikus,

WAYNE-DANIEL BERARD

A distant chatter of hammers

high up on towers

outside of time itself

Session 7

Today I discussed with Sylvia my desire to begin seeing "where all this is going," to get some sense of what this regression experience may be telling me about the present life, and where it might be calling me about the rest of my (present) life. Of course, we both agreed that we just had to see how it went, but I felt a bit better venting that (minor but growing) frustration.

Sylvia led me into meditation. I began to see a kind of pulsating, round mass in the upper right of my field of vision (eyes closed). It seemed to be kind of going in and out, and there were wavy areas around and across it, like ripples. As the scene began to concretize, I could see it was the sun, very large and orange/red; there were thin ripples of clouds all around it and some passed in front of it. I seemed to be looking at the scene from a distance; there were sand dunes and smallish pyramids; I realized this was the place I had seen before, the place I would come to walk, think and be alone. At the bottom left of the scene, I could see The Egyptian master on the left and Yossi to his right. Yossi had his tallit over his head like a hood and was swaying back and forth; the Egyptian had his arms lifted. Then there was shift, and I was experiencing all this from Yossi's point of view. The Egyptian master and I were praying together as the sun was rising. I couldn't understand the words he used, although I did know some Egyptian. It seemed like a much older form.

It came time for silent, personal prayer. I wrapped the tallit across my face and swayed. I asked God to please help me with "my feelings for La'nah," that I loved her but didn't know what to do about it. I asked that I not "make a mess out of all this." When we had finished, we began walking back, across the fine sand, toward a little dirt road and to a wooden bridge over a canal. The Egyptian master asked how I was doing with everything. I told him that I just wished I could speak with La'nah, that her mother was usually present during our tutoring. He smiled and said he thought he might be able to help.

The scene shifted. I was back in my cell. I was standing over a table with a scroll rolled out on it; it was written in Greek, but was very sloppy, with letters unevenly sized and even some cross-outs. There was a knock; it was the Egyptian master; he was so tall that he had to duck to get through the door. He said it was "all arranged"; I could meet with La'nah alone that night! I should get to her house "three hours after the moon had risen," and walk around the back of the garden wall. I asked him how I was going to get in, as the wall had no gate, and the garden could only be entered from the house. He gave a joking little smile and told me not to worry about it, but just to go to the back wall. (I didn't particularly like the smile and felt like I was being put on a little).

WAYNE-DANIEL BERARD

Night came. I walked through the square with the fountain, through the market area (all quiet), over the arched stone bridge. All the boats were tied up and still. Then down the cobblestone street to the house. I stopped there, looked around, then went around to the back. There was a crescent moon that night, but it was very bright. I could see a big mound of dirt piled up against the wall; beside it was a good-sized hole. Someone had dug up this dirt and laid it there; it was sort of orangey in color. Apparently, this was to help me get over the wall. There was still about 4 feet left from the top of the mound to the top of the wall. I tried to climb the mound, but the dirt was loose and like clay; it was somewhat slippery, and I slid down twice before I made it to the top. My white clothes were also all covered with orange clay. At the top, I tried jumping and grabbing a hold of the top of the wall. It took me a couple of times, but I pulled my chest up over the top. I could see that I was right over the spot where the water spouted through a stone face in the wall, so I tried to inch myself over on my arms to the left. Then I pulled my right leg over and swung myself so that I was now hanging over the inside, my chest and arms on the top of the wall (which was very gritty, like stucco). I then let go and let myself drop; I came down kind of hard on my feet, but then fell back on my butt. I felt embarrassed and hoped that La'nah wasn't there yet; she wasn't. I brushed myself off as best I could and hid in some bushes near the table and benches where we usually studied. I waited for what seemed forever, but it was probably more like 5–10 minutes. Finally, I heard a rustling and she came out. She looked beautiful! She had a long red robe on with a red wrap; both had gold-colored filigree running through them. I stepped out of the bushes; she saw me and came forward. We each stopped very close to each other; neither of us seemed to know what to do next. My heart was pounding so hard and my stomach felt a little sick. Then La'nah took a step forward and *held me! She was little (shorter than Christine) and her head was pressed to my chest. I had never felt anything so wonderful (actually, I had never been held before, ever!). She was just so warm and soft and real. Everything just filled up inside me; the whole world melted away. I felt so happy; I realized that I hadn't really known "happy" before, but just thought that how I'd been living was all there was. I knew I loved La'nah so much and that I couldn't live without her, without this feeling. I remember thinking to myself, "What good is all the knowledge without this?" We pushed back a little from each other; I looked down into her face and those big brown eyes. Then she closed her eyes and moved her head forward; we kissed (just lips, but very **WOW!**). Everything spun; I felt my whole life turning inside out and I didn't care. I knew I had to be with this girl, that I would ask to marry her.*

After the kiss, she looked up at me and said, very hushed, "I love you, Yossi ben . . ." She stopped. "I don't even know your whole name," she said. "Who were your parents?" I felt like someone had stabbed me right in the chest. I said, "I don't have any parents." I motioned that we should sit down on one of the benches. La'nah was holding both of my hands in her hands. So, then I told her about everything: the fire, the desert, being found, Dothan, Ruth, the new master, the academy, leaving to come to Egypt, etc. I tried very hard not to induce any pity from her, but every so often I'd hear her catch her breath. When I was done, I said, "So now you know. I don't even have a name to give you. I don't have anything." She took my two hands and put them to the upper part of her chest, just over her breasts (I had never touched a woman before, except for that one aborted hug before leaving Amma). She looked right at me and said, "This will be our name now." She said "our." There was a little pause. I said I'd always been alone, that I didn't know how to do anything else. She said, "No more alone. No more alone,"—twice, just like that. Then I said that I wanted to "speak with her father." La'nah said, "I think you should have Pote speak with him. But it's my mother who I'm concerned about." When I asked her why, she said that I wasn't "a believer." I didn't know what to say. Then La'nah suggested that I go to a service with them, that this might help. She said I could just watch. I agreed.

We stood up, and we held each other again. I never wanted to let go, ever. She gave me a little kiss on the lips, turned around and hurried inside. I was left alone in the garden. I hated being alone. I wanted to run inside and grab her and just run away somewhere with her. I knew then that I couldn't live without her, that I couldn't keep on in the way I'd been going, no matter how "sacred" it was. I felt kind of guilty about it, but there it was.

Then I looked around and realized that I didn't have a way out of this garden! I took the two benches and tried not to make any noise. I placed one on the other against the back wall and climbed on them. This left me with even more space to reach up to than previously. I jumped up and barely held on; I pulled myself up, swung around. I was too far over for the dirt pile. I just let go and hit hard. But I was okay; I got up and walked back the way I'd come.

The most telling part of this regression was hearing the voice of La'nah—my being literally saved by her words and her tone, her facial expression and her touch.

THE LAST ESSENE

Of course, I recognized them all in the person, the voice, the manner of my Lovely Christine, and in the way she had assured me into love, in both lifetimes.

I remember so well the first time I introduced Christine to Rabbi Alan. To say that they hit it off would be like saying David Ortiz was a career bunter! They laughed together and talked about everything (not just me). As we were leaving, my dear teacher Alan who had been my dear teacher Ishmael/Elisha said to me, "I have one simple instruction for you: Be led by Christine in all things!"

It was the best advice I've ever received (and something that Christine would good-naturedly never let me forget!).

After Yossi finally shared with La'nah the story of his life—of orphaning and homelessness, of separation and rejection—she responded, not with pity, not even with reassurances. Her response was herself, pluralizing—a life moving from "mine" to "our." I can still feel the incredulity, the complete and joyous unexpectedness of La'nah, of Christine:

all along

I wake up with

a start every

morning, surprised

to be here, then I

turn and see you,

my great and only-

needed love, my

constant occasion,

you've managed it

again, I'd no idea

today was my

surprise party,

the dark merely

part of love's

plan all along.

I found Christine after I'd found my Jewishness and Jewish Renewal; Yossi found La'nah after he'd found, and was struggling with, a much broader Jewish universe than his Essenic conditioning had prepared him for. His experiences with Ishmael/Elisha and at the Bridge Academy had opened him intellectually, but none of it had touched his heart—a part of him that he barely wished to acknowledge existed.

In La'nah, Yossi could finally bring all that it meant for him to be a Jew—body, mind, and heart—into one integrated life, fully alive at all levels. La'nah, he was coming to see, was literally the *bat kol*, the Divine Voice, the key in which the symphony of his life had always been played, and the thematic resolution of all the movements of that symphony. Even the growing sectarianism of that time, embodied by La'nah's mother, could not stand in the way of this fulfillment.

In Christine, I had come to see the sense and the purpose of a life so variegated, in many ways so contradictory and senseless. She was that defining moment in my life, my constant occasion of meaning and of openness to what was yet unknown.

In Judaism, the defining moment happens at Mt. Sinai, when the Jewish people are offered the Torah by God. It is maintained, in the mystical viewpoint, that all Jews throughout history, past, present, and future, were present at this event.

The Telling
        ('haggadah')

                When I stood

(as did every Jew)

                at the foot of Mt. Sinai,

                and the mountain smoked

WAYNE-DANIEL BERARD

and the trumpets blared
thunder,

I heard the ten speakings
(the Hebrew doesn't command)

and said (with everyone else)
"Let us not hear God's voice
further
lest we die . . ."

So I picked up
my armful of shalts and shalt
nots,

and headed for the desert,

too scared to listen,
preferring to be told.

Forty years (plus some)
of wandering, thirsting,
obeying,

THE LAST ESSENE

and breaking finally,

I looked up and
cursed circles.

Same mountain,

only now dying
seemed a preferential option.

Trumpets,
thunder,

alone

I heard God's
further voice;

Christine,

it spoke

your name.

WAYNE-DANIEL BERARD

I recognized, there in the chair in Sylvia's office, that defining moment, that integrational happening, that creation of the personality who would be Wayne-Daniel in the liberation of the Essene who was Yossi son of No One, whose true name would thereafter be Yossi Lev La'nah—Yossi, La'nah's Heart. Just as mine was and is Wayne-Daniel, In All Things, Christine's.

CHAPTER 12

Forebodings?

This book opened with my notes on the seventh of my regression sessions with Sylvia, the one which detailed my first experience as Yossi of a shabbat service in a Christos (Jesus Jews) community. The next week, Christine and I returned to Sylvia's office for the next session.

Session 8

After exchanging pleasantries, Sylvia led me into the meditation. I could feel myself going deep rather quickly; actually, "deep" is really the right word. I almost immediately had a sense of being down inside something, looking up. I could see a shining disc in the upper center of my field of vision; after a few seconds, things became clearer. I seemed to be down deep in some sort of shaft; it was round, and I could make out stonework in the dark. I was up almost to my knees in some sort of dark, musty muck, very cold and wet. There was a rope that I'd sort of wrapped the left side of my body and left arm around; my feet were standing on something sort of thin and wobbly that was down submerged in the muck. In my right hand I was holding a stick, like a walking stick. But I could also see a glint of something yellow, like brass or gold, on the top of the stick. It was dark in there, but the object looked something like a letter "T" with droopy arms. I didn't know where I was or what I was doing there; when I looked up, I could see that small disk of light at the top, maybe 20 feet up above me.

Then, suddenly, the scene shifted. I knew that I was seeing something from earlier. I was standing by what seemed to be an old well, but it was very odd looking. The rocks that formed it were just laid on each other in a loose circle; they weren't very high, maybe 2 ½–3 feet from the ground. Next to it was a very strangely shaped pole; it looked like something out of a Dr. Seuss book. It started at the ground next to the circle of stones; the butt end of the pole was wedged into a stone in the ground with an indentation in it. Then the pole arced up and over the opening of the well in a big curve. A rough-hewn support (it looked like the "V" of two branches joining) came up from the ground and the curved pole rested on it; its curve dipped down toward the well's face, and a rope hung from it. (I assume there was a bucket on the end of the rope). If you wanted water, you'd push the end of the pole out of its catch, then lower the entire arc down into the well. But I knew somehow that this was an old well that we hadn't used for a very long time; we got our water from the fountain in the square behind the school compound. I was standing beside the well, talking to Pote, the Egyptian Master. He was saying that La'nah's father had agreed to the marriage! I felt wonderful. But then he said that the father wished us to wait a year! I was crestfallen, a whole year? Why a year? Pote just smiled that knowing (and annoying!) little smile and said that La'nah was only 13! She would be 14 in a few weeks. Her family was concerned about the health risk of her possibly having babies so young. 13!!! I'd had no idea; she didn't look that young. I felt rather stupid and embarrassed. Pote said he'd arranged for me to visit with La'nah once a week during that year, chaperoned, of course. I thanked him and hoped to myself that the servant, Cush, would be the chaperone, as he already seemed sympathetic to us.

The scene shifted again. I was sitting in the garden with La'nah, in the same spot as the night I'd snuck in. Again, she was holding both of my hands in her hands. She looked so beautiful; I loved looking into her eyes. I just want to live forever in those eyes. She has on a purple-lilac colored robe, it has little fuchsia-colored lines running through it. We don't say much; we just look at each other. I don't want to say anything about her age; I don't want to embarrass her. She reaches around behind her on the bench and says she has a gift for me from her mother. It's a brass piece, looking like a "T" with droopy arms; it's on a round, brass stand. The whole thing's about 5 inches high. I know that it's the Greek letter "Tau." La'nah says that it is a sign for the Christos, as it looks like a cross. But Tau is also the last letter of the Hebrew aleph bait, (although it doesn't look like this) and means "finality" and "completion." The Egyptians, she says, also use Tau. La'nah says that it shows that her mother approves of our marriage. She'd like it if I became Christoi, but knows the letter has other meanings. La'nah likes that it means "fulfillment" and "endings," as we'll be together forever now. I decide to take the piece and have it fitted to the top of my master's old walking stick. I start to lean in to kiss La'nah, but I hear Cush clearing his throat from across the garden.

The feeling of dark muck that I experienced in this regression was all too familiar to me. As a matter in fact, it had become so intense and pervasive that I had sought out psychotherapy because of it.

I had been seeing my amazing therapist, Eve Goldfarb, even before I was named Director of Spiritual Life and Chaplain of my college. Although she was quite open to past-life regression, she did not use it in her own work, and even if she had, the boundaries of her profession would have kept her from doing a presentation on it for me at school. But I had faithfully included my work with Sylvia in Eve's and my meetings together; in fact, the session notes which form the heart of this book were initially written for that purpose.

What had brought me to Eve was a phenomenon which I had come to call "The Ooze."

Imagine yourself being filled up from the base of your spine, up through your gut and lower organs—a dark, tarry, pitch of a feeling, rising steadily through your chest cavity, over your heart, thickly flooding your mind and senses with a hopeless, deadening ooze.

This ooze had a nature and a message—it was the dense, black certainty that you were completely unlovable, long-term. That there was something fundamentally wrong with you that kept love from ever being a part of your life for long. That, sooner or later,

THE LAST ESSENE

regardless of person or promise, you would be irredeemably and utterly alone.

This ooze had been growing in me for months if not years. I came by it naturally.

Every adopted child, I think, asks themselves what must have been wrong with them, that their mother gave them away; no amount of assurance to the contrary, not even finding one's birth-mother and hearing of her circumstances, can fill this hole in that very young part of their soul. Add to this an adopted circumstance of misplacement—of being so entirely different from one's adopted family and surroundings as to be alien, even existentially threatening. An extraordinarily empathetic and compassionate male child, intellectually gifted, athletically hopeless, and spiritually oriented to his core had no business in the bare knuckled, envy-and-resentment-filled, lower-economic class environment in which I was placed. That which I essentially was, was held in lowest disdain. I believe my adopted parents were relieved when I chose seminary at fourteen; perhaps someone like me belonged in the Church. I certainly did not belong with them.

As an adult, I would create poetry out of this experience:

WAYNE-DANIEL BERARD

Jewish Child, Indirect Adoption

    Lily

    the miniature

    daschund

    chasing

    disks,

    balls,

    a stick,

    snaps

    invariably,

    their imaginary

    necks

    with a

        toss of

    her angelic

    head.

No one

    told her

to do this.

THE LAST ESSENE

When he'd read

their Book

entire

by fifth

      grade,

the parents

marveled

as they

backed away.

Despite

his size,

he'd strike

only out

prone to

WAYNE-DANIEL BERARD

travel

    he'd stubbornly

    rebound.

    Never

    picked for

    (only on),

    he wouldn't

    just vanish,

    showing up

insistently

where other

children belonged

fumbling.

No one

knew,

not the parents

normally

THE LAST ESSENE

parochial,

not the relatives

unusually

tolerant

of the constant

thoughts, sounds

      they

couldn't follow,

as of a sincere

      animal

      they'd reach over

      and pat

call him good,

not the nuns

who assumed

some secret calling,

a priestly destiny,

a birth sealed,

not their

WAYNE-DANIEL BERARD

    angel

    miniatures

who

    chased him

    after Good

    Friday service,

    snapped

    his head

    back with

    each blow,

    left him

    out

    cold

    without

    a thought,

    a sound.

    No one

    told them

    to do this,

they just

knew.

It seemed, oddly enough, that my finding, falling in love with, and marrying my lovely Christine had actually exacerbated the Ooze. It was quite the contradiction; on the one hand I was deeply, overwhelmingly happy, more so than I had ever been. On the other, the Ooze constantly rose up to flood me in the dank assurance that it was only a matter of time before Christine realized that any sort of love involving me was doomed from the start. Sooner or later, she and I would just fall apart.

When Eve delved deeper into these feelings with me, what emerged led directly to God—or at least to my version of same. It became clear that I seemed to feel singled out to be God's and God's alone, that there would be allowed no place or room in my life for any other, more human form of love. I was "set apart" from all that, by nature and calling meant to be a lone figure in relationship solely with the Divine, pressing my nose up against the glass of "ordinary life," including love, but never being admitted into it for long. Imagine Gandalf with a prayer life.

Where did this Ooze come from? Yes, my earlier life had been little short of abysmal, but this phenomenon seemed to be linked specifically to romantic love and long-term relationship; I never felt any sense of inescapable, lonely failure about my professional life or my writing, for instance? As Eve and I continued our work together, I realized that the Ooze had never manifested itself about my *first* marriage, either, and that had ended in divorce! No, this dark, seductively depressing anticipation of sure isolation was solely about Christine and me. Why?

I was about to find out.

The scene changes. I'm in the quarters of the Greek-Jewish master; this looks like sort of an ancient version of an office. There's a heavy table with scrolls and some little statues; the master stand behind it. His name is Philotides. Somehow, I know that he is the son of Philo, the philosopher—the illegitimate son. This is why he did not inherit his father's school; he founded this one instead. He's older, mid- to late-sixties. He's losing his hair, and brushes some of the long strands across the bald top of his head! He seems very serious-looking. I'm making my pitch to him about having Marcella teach at the school. Pote is there, too, on the other side of the desk, back to my left, leaning against a wall with his arms folded across his chest, smiling. He's enjoying me being nervous, making my case. I tell Philotides that there is growing interest in the teachings of the Christos, and that there are also many wealthy, (home) educated women who would like to study and could add revenue to the school. I tell him about Marcella, about who her father was. He asks where the women would study, as it would be too much of a distraction for them to study in the compound with the men. I asked if perhaps there was property we could acquire or rent nearby; I'm sure that the revenue from the new women students would off-set this. He says that there does happen to be such a place, just across the square from the school. It's a villa that was willed to him by

THE LAST ESSENE

a student. But someone would have to be in charge there, a man, to oversee the teaching and the "proper actions" of the women. Of course, he says, it would have to be a married man; as a matter of fact, "the place would make the perfect home for a newly married couple . . ." Then Philotides starts to smile, and Pote laughs. Philotides reaches across the desk and takes my lower arm in his hand and I do the same for his—this must be some sort of handshake. So, it was all decided beforehand! I should have known that Pote would speak to him about this first and lay the groundwork for me and warn me of any difficulties.

So, Marcella comes to teach. The villa is beautiful; there's a big open room in the center of it; about 9–10 women come to study—some Jews, some Greeks and Romans, some Egyptians (much darker than the others). I observe, but after a time just come in and out, to say that I've checked. I can see Marcella is doing well. We've gotten to know each other; there's a sadness about her, as she never married or had children. She says that her father's work is her life, but she still seems sad. I like her; she's the first woman I've had a non-romantic friendship with.

The scene shifts again. It's La'nah's and my wedding. It's held in the garden at her father's house. Her mother had wanted it in the Christoi synagogue, and her father had wanted it in the Roman temple. So, they had it at home. My friend, Yoachanan, leads the service. La'nah is all in white, with a white shawl cowled over her head. She's so incredibly beautiful; I'm so happy. I never knew I could be this happy. We say to each other, "I love you forever." She loves me. The school is supportive of me. Everything is so good.

Then it's nighttime. We're upstairs in the villa, lying together in our bed. It's warm; we just have a light sheet over us. We're not dressed. I'm on La'nah's right; I lean over toward her face and put my hand on her cheek. I'm nervous (of course!), but I'm also worried about her age and a possible pregnancy. I say, "Maybe we should wait." I can feel her stiffen; I hurry to tell her why I said this. I can feel her relaxing again next to me. She reaches up her right hand and puts it to my cheek. She says, "You worry too much." Then she pulls me close to her. I can feel her up against me. I've never felt anything so overwhelmingly wonderful.

Next I find myself back at the school. I'm continuing to invite new people to teach; this has become part of my role. I send Cush across the big lake that bounds one side of the city; on the other side there are two communities, one male, one female. They live in the desert and devote their time to learning, especially about numbers and anything to do with mathematics. They believe that everything can be reduced to numbers. Cush has two parchments from me, inviting representatives from each community to come and teach. The lake is very big; it takes him a day each way to cross. When he gets back, he tells me that he delivered both parchments to the male community, as he wasn't allowed in the females'. There was no immediate message back. A few days seem to go by. I'm in my quarters, looking at the rather sloppy Greek manuscript; this is a copy of Marcella's father's work. There's a knock, but before I can say anything Pote walks in. He says I should come outside and "see something." I step out and there are two figures standing there, one shorter than the other. They are women, both wrapped tight in white cloths with white head scarves and scarves across their lower faces; they look like Bedouins (or

THE LAST ESSENE

ninjas!). *The smaller one hands Pote a parchment; it says that they are "Pythagoreans," that no one from the men's community was coming, but that they wished to teach. I think this is wonderful, but ask Pote where they'll live? He says they can live with the "Hestians"—somehow, I know that these are celibate women who always keep a sacred fire burning to a special Goddess for women. The two can live with them and walk back and forth to the villa. Pote and I ask the women (who seem to prefer silence) if they'd like to come with us to see the Greek-Jewish Master or to go inside my quarters, out of the sun. But they shake their heads; they'll stand right there (apparently) until we get back.*

Another shift. I'm in the yard of the compound, walking toward its upper right-hand corner. In front of the quarters there is a very little man, very skinny and old. He is draped in an orange robe over one shoulder and sits in a full lotus. He is a disciple of the Buddha, and came to Egypt as a young boy, as part of a delegation from the Indian king. He is the only one of that group still alive; people would come to him for advice and study in the Egyptian Quarter. When I heard of him from Pote I spent some time with him, and then invited him to teach and spend his old age at the school. We call him "Yodi"—"yod" is the smallest letter in the aleph bait. No one can pronounce his Indian name, but I get the idea that "Yodi" sounds like "yogi." I like him very much; we often sit and talk. He tells me about the dangers of desire. I tell him that all desire can't be bad; I desire La'nah, after all. He says that desire of a man for a woman is natural but warns me against "desiring too much."

My research would later show me that Pythagoreans and Buddhists did exist in the Egypt of this period.

It's a wonderful experience when the outsides of things and the insides of things come together, when they match up.

As Yossi, I had begun a process to open the Bridge even wider, to carry the work of my Master, Rabbi Ishmael/Elisha, even farther than he was able to in his besieged lifetime. I was actually lobbying to have a Jew of the Jesus School of Judaism (remember, the split had not yet occurred) teach in our Academy—and not just any Christoi, but a woman! Granted, she was the daughter of none other than the first of the canonical Evangelists, John Mark, later known as St. Mark, the boon companion of the author of most of New Testament, St. Paul. But even such "creds" would hardly overcome, for most, the barrier of her gender—not to mention the fact that she was a leader in a brand of Judaism many saw as heretical. Still, Yossi pressed forward.

The regression seemed to show that the two founders of the school, Pote and Philotides, had already come to their own (favorable) conclusion about Yossi's proposal. In retrospect, this is hardly surprising. Pote we have already seen to have been faithful to spiritual expressions repressed and persecuted for over a thousand years. Philotides, my regression had shown me, was the "illegitimate" son of Philo of Alexandria, *the* preeminent Hellenized Jewish scholar of his day (and, interestingly enough, an expert on Essenes). It was clear that he could inherit nothing of the Academy his father founded and ran, due to his "illegitimate" status. Did that make him more amenable to Yossi, the orphan raised by Essenes? It would have been commonly understood that my abandonment on the Essenes' doorstep back in the 1st century meant that I was either "illegitimate" myself or that one or both of my parents were dead, with no family willing or able to raise me.

Additionally, could this have had anything to do with Philotides' openness to a follower of the Christos teaching in his Academy? There had been a cloud over Jesus' life, as well, as there was a question of his being conceived out of wedlock; Torah forbids acceptance of such individuals, *mamzerim* in the Hebrew, "into God's congregation even to the tenth generation." (Dt 23:3). Nothing could be proven in the case of Jesus, but a close reading of the Gospels will show that the stigma of even the possibility never left him. (Talmud, commentaries on Torah and Jewish life, leave little doubt what it believed on this score and the negative light in which this cast Jesus).

This may be difficult for we post-moderns to comprehend, but even in my lifetime the "taint of illegitimacy" was a very real thing. In 1965, when the Franciscan Vocation Director came for the "home visit," the experience was going very well—until my father asked me to go to my room so he could "speak with Father privately." It wasn't until many years later that I learned the reason: My father had heard that children born out of wedlock could not become priests! I guess the Director just laughed and said, "Maybe in the Middle Ages!" I was admitted without a hitch.

I cannot help but believe that it was the combined experience of these three men—a devotee of a forbidden faith, a scholar cast out by his own people to the tenth generation of his progeny, and the orphaned last Essene—that would ultimately expand the range of their Bridge Academy. With a faculty including women, Christoi, Pythagoreans, and Buddhists, it would be the most open, the most pluralistic center for spiritual learning in Alexandria, if not in the known world. And, therefore, the most despised, as well.

So much for the "outsides." But what of the "insides"?

Because Marcella would be teaching only women (one step at a time!), a suitable venue needed to be found, one outside the all-male Academy grounds. This led to the use of a villa owned by Philotides—but it was still the 2nd century CE! No matter how progressive for the times, the entire enterprise would need to be overseen by a male, but of course a married male. Soon it becomes clear to Yossi that another purpose is at work here beyond liberated academics—as an Essene, Yossi would have no personal finances, and his only home was his quarters at the Academy. How could he possibly marry La'nah under such circumstances? In deference to the pacifist Essene, let us say that his friends found a way to free two birds with one swoop? Yossi and La'nah could live in the villa; Marcella's classes would be duly "overseen"—*b'osher v'osher!*— "happily ever after!" (Hebrew)

Even La'nah's mother had seemed to have gotten into the interfaith spirit! Her gift to her future son-in-law of a Tau-shaped brass handle for his Master's walking stick (with the many meanings associated with that letter) signaled not just her acceptance of Yossi, but a victory of pluralism over exclusivism, of Love over narrowness.

The "outsides" of multiculturalism and openness of spirit seem to have made it possible for the "insides" of an orphaned Essene and a half-Christoi Jew/half-Roman girl to join together in love.

Eighteen centuries later, the great author (and reincarnationist) Hermann Hesse would write:

> *"Similar to Jesus or the Buddha is anyone who,*
> *touched by one of the magical truths,*
> *ceases to distinguish between thinking and living."*

CHAPTER 13

Now It's Now Again

The scene shifts. La'nah is pregnant! Everyone is very happy; I'm also a little worried about her age. Pote has Egyptian physicians coming in to see her. La'nah's mother comes to stay, and many of the women from the Christoi often come to help, including Marcella. It's night, and I'm sleeping in my school quarters. Apparently, there's some sort of custom or superstition about the husband being around the woman during the final days of her pregnancy; it's only supposed to be women. So, I'm sleeping at the school. All of a sudden, I smell smoke. I shake myself awake. There it is; I smell it again. And I hear voices, angry voices. Am I dreaming? Remembering? No, I'm fully awake now. I throw on some clothes and partially open my door.

Down at the gate, a crowd is swarming through—there must be 80 people, maybe more, all Jews. They're yelling and cursing. They have big sticks and clubs and torches. They're setting the place on fire! They jump on anyone who comes out of their quarters, teachers, servants, older students who assist their masters. I slam my door shut. God, this can't be happening again! What do I do? Is La'nah alright? How can I get out to her? There are so many of them. I open my door again and *get down on my stomach. I have the stick with the brass Tau. I crawl along toward the Egyptian Master's quarters; he'll know what to do. As I go along, I hit the well. I look up; they're coming closer, faster. Yelling and screaming and burning and clubbing people. I'll never make it across the yard. I push at the bottom of the pole with the butt of my hand; it dislodges. I very cautiously sit myself on the stone rim; I grab hold of the rope and set my feet on each side of the bucket. Then I oomph myself over and in. The bucket and rope and I plummet down. I hit the bottom; it's all this dark ooze. It smells like rotted vegetation, very moldy. I can taste it in my mouth. I sink up to just below my knees; if I wasn't standing on the bucket, I'd get sucked in and suffocate. I just hold on, looking up. I can hear people shouting; some are crying out in pain. I can smell smoke and hear big "pops!" I can't believe I'm here again. I should be helping, doing something. But I know there are too many of them. I'll just wait here until it's safe, and I'll pull myself up and go to La'nah.*

On and on the time goes. I can feel great heat, even down here. The whole place must be on fire. I try to hold on, try not to fall asleep. Morning comes. I don't hear anything else. I try to pull myself up the rope, but my hands are all slimy and slippery. I can't get up. My legs are killing me from all this standing, and I'm so cold in this muck. I begin to yell as loud as I can for help, but no one answers or comes. I pull and pull on the rope; the pole clatters against the support, but nobody sees it or hears. God, I've got to get out of here. I can't die in this place. What about La'nah? The baby? I keep trying and trying all day. It gets terribly hot down here. My voice is giving out; I don't dare try drinking any of this muck. Night comes again. I feel so hopeless; I'm filling up with despair inside. Then I see light begin to come at the top of the well. Morning again. I try to call out; I shake the pole with the rope. Then I hear someone calling back. It seems somewhat far away. I try to shout back; I pull on the rope. Then I can see a form at the top. "Pull me up," I try to shout, but I'm only croaking. The rope begins to move; I go up a few feet, then I drop back down. I'm heavy. I beg the person to keep trying. I take the stick and shove it in my clothes; I try to help push up against wall of the well with my right hand. Now I'm going up. Near the top, I take out the stick; I hold it up by the brass end. "Grab it! Grab it!" I shout. Then I'm up. My head and shoulders are over the rim; my stomach is scraping the stones. I tumble over onto the ground. It's Cush, faithful, good Cush. I can barely talk, I'm so thirsty. I ask him what happened. He says there are riots in the Jewish Quarter; the Jews are rioting. They feel that they are badly treated. It even spilled over into other quarters. It had been simmering for months. Hadn't I known it? But I'd been all taken up with a new wife and a baby coming, my new mission at the school. I say to him, "But these were all Jews! Why did they do this to us?" I can see around me that the school has been burnt; I can see bodies on the ground. Cush says that traditional Jews hate the school (his words are "real Jews"). It has "too much newness"; they think it's polluted, heretical. That word again!

I want to get up, but I can hardly move my legs. I tell him I have to get to La'nah. I try to crawl toward the gate; Cush stops me. There are tears running down his face. He says that La'nah and her mother were trapped in the Jewish Quarter. They're both dead. The villa has been burned. Yesterday, her father finally fought his way across the bridge with his soldiers; he took their bodies back to the Roman Quarter.

I can't believe it! It can't be true! I turn and try to crawl back to the well. I want to throw myself in; "Just let me die here, will you!" I'm crying (in the chair as well) and sobbing and trying to crawl back. I

THE LAST ESSENE

get to the edge; my head and shoulder are over, but Cush has me by the back of my clothes. He won't let go. He's yelling for me to stop. Finally, he pulls me back; I don't have enough strength. I just lie there and sob and shake. What will I do now? How will I live now, without La'nah? And the baby, no baby. Cush says, "You are the son-in-law of the governor's aide. He'll take care of you. We have to get you back there." I just give up. I'll do whatever he says. He tries to help me up; my legs are stiff and weak from all that standing in the well. They're covered in muck up to the knees. I lean with my left hand on the stick with the brass Tau; I let Cush support me under my right arm (he's short). Together we walk toward the gate; one door is totally off and lying on the ground, the other is hanging by one (upper) hinge. There are bodies all over the ground, but I don't see Pote or Philotides or the Indian Master. Together we limp out the gate, down the little alley, into the square. The fountain is still running; how can that be? The villa is all caved in on itself and charred; all the buildings look like this. Cush turns me away from it and toward the canal and the stone bridge.

At this point, Sylvia asks me to stop and to try to put this "tape back in the box." I'm an absolute mess, a wreck. She is very concerned that I "come back to this life," to Wayne-Daniel, August 6th, 2007." We spend a good amount of time on this "coming back" process. Finally, she invites me to open my eyes when I'm ready. I look at the clock and it's noon; we started at 10:30. I asked Sylvia about this, and she said she'd thought it would just be "cruelty" to have stopped at an hour. My insides feel all battered. I just want to go home with Christine, just back to my regular life. "This is now," Sylvia keeps saying. I just keep looking at Christine. "This is now," I keep saying to myself. And we leave.

I have been sitting at my laptop for several minutes, trying to muster up the strength to write about this particular phase of my regression. Just rereading the notes has brought it all back with near-agonizing clarity. In a life that has known its share of suffering, those ninety minutes were among the most excruciating I'd ever experienced.

La'nah was dead. The woman who would be my Lovely Christine was murdered by a mob, along with our unborn child. Yossi had walked away from an entire way of life, his very definition of himself and the world, to be with this woman—or, to put it more accurately, he had accomplished the Herculean task of *dragging* another whole half of the Universe, the part consisting of Love, Warmth, and Empathy, to the sure, intellectual hemisphere of Pure Reason. It had been like pushing two powerful magnets together; they seemed to resist each other by their very nature (just as he'd been told). But finally, the unity in apparent opposites had emerged. Reason and faith now studied together; righteousness of mind and rightness of heart had kissed each other. In the persons of Yossi and La'nah, that opposing magnetism had snapped together in a lover's embrace, as inseparable as they had for so long seemed impossibly conflicted.

Was this why I had resisted my feelings for Christine so much at the beginning? Once before I had put aside the coldly secure safety of Masculine Intellectuality. Once before, I had moved beyond the Small Kingdom of Complete Sense into the moonlit garden of Solomon's Song. And, rather than Light and Warmth coming together in a life measured in thank yous, Mind and Heart had exploded upon contact, like Matter and Anti-Matter trying to waltz away a completely incendiary oppositeness.

So, this was where the Ooze came from? A sense-memory from eighteen-hundred years before, a warning as to what happens when you dare disturb the Universe (to quote Eliot) and attempt to join together that which should only be kept asunder? The felt and the reasoned? Love and Truth? Yossi/Wayne-Daniel and anybody?

Jewish riots in Alexandria and throughout the Near East were historical realities of the time. They were collectively called the Kitos War, and occurred between the two major Jewish rebellions against Rome, The Great Revolt which had seen the destruction of Yossi's first home, and the Bar Kochba rebellion, which would end in the utter destruction of the ancient Jewish homeland and the diaspora of the Jewish people.

Such would be a dispassionately intellectual description of these happenings. For Yossi, they were the end of the world, a collapse of a mindset and of the heart's promise. The forces of exclusivity and narrowness had won; the Bridge Academy with its openness and pluralism lay in smoldering ruins at his feet. God only knew what had become of Pote and Philotides, Marcella, the Buddhist Master, and the Pythagorean women. God and Yossi both knew what had become La'nah and her unborn child. All Yossi wanted to do was to retreat back into the Ooze, permanently.

I would come to see in this regression session the power of past-life trauma to affect one's present life. Christine and I had decided not to have children together; we had each come into our relationship with three already. Christine was in excellent health, and there was very little reasonable chance of my losing her in this way. But the Ooze I was experiencing did not deal with possible physical loss, a la Yossi and La'nah; it sought to convince me of what the last Essene had had to move beyond—the idea that being close to God and close to a romantic partner was incompatible, that the two states were mutually exclusive. Of course, La'nah had had to go; Yossi's future progress with God depended on it. And of course, Christine would one day leave me—and leave me free to continue the necessarily lonely path of those close to the Divine.

I so did not want this to be true! The thought of a life without my Great Love was every bit as devastating in the 21st century as it was in the 2nd.

I remember walking up the stairs after this session (Sylvia's office was in the lower level of her home). Christine had to ask me to stop periodically, as I was swaying, disoriented. We came out onto the lawn and Christine had me take off my sandals and walk barefoot in the grass. She knew I needed to reground myself to the earth, to the earth of today, that moment.

"This is now," Sylvia had repeated to me after this session, and I had repeated these words to myself. But what did "now" mean, in this context?

As devastating as this particular session had been, I was already anxious to come back. I needed to know what Yossi had done next.

What could the person I had once been show the person I was now about the person I could yet become?

CHAPTER 14

To Be, Become, and End

Session 9

Sylvia, I, and Christine spent a bit of time discussing last week's session, its intensity, and my reaction to it. I spoke about a feeling of coming near a close to this past life's experience and what might come next in terms of processing and exploring what it all means. Apparently, one can follow the life all the way through to its death and one's "time" in the "between state," where much of this processing occurs. Sylvia asked if, with the academic year starting soon, I felt a need to move somewhat faster in terms of my own schedule's constraints. Luckily, my schedule is good, and, although I am anxious to see where this is all going, I have no wish to rush the process.

I then went into meditation, like usual. In about 2–3 minutes, pyramidic shapes began to concretize, and soon I was seeing a scene: There were several pyramids sort of bunched together; in the foreground, I saw a figure standing, facing in my direction. She was very covered, even most of her face, but I could tell by the height and posture (a bit tall for a woman of the times and hunched a little at the shoulders) and the strong sense of melancholy about her that this was Marcella. The scene began to draw back and widen out; I could see a low, flat ship, like a barge, on the river. I could see Yossi sitting in the stern on a plank drawn across the end of the ship. Up farther, near the front, La'nah's father was standing; he looked very serious and dour. He was in his military clothing, including a breastplate and a red cape (but no helmet). He just looked straight ahead, over the river. There were two or three women also on board (I think they were servants) and men standing with long poles. Across the ship, on the opposite side from Cornelius, Cush was standing. He held a brass box in his hands; it was about the shape and size of a fairly large toolbox. Its sides slanted upward like a roof but flattened at the top. On those slanted panels there were lots and lots of tiny holes, like in a cheese grater. Cush stepped forward and stood next to Cornelius; he was short, so Cornelius was able to look right over him toward Yossi. Then he nodded, as if to say, "Okay to go on?"

At this time, the point of view changed. Now I was Yossi and looking out through his eyes. I knew that the box contained the ashes of La'nah and her mother. I felt entirely empty and spent. I felt like I was dead already, like a big, hollow bell that someone had struck, and now there was just the reverberation inside, back and forth in the emptiness. I knew La'nah wasn't in that box. I didn't care what they did with the ashes. I nodded back to my father-in-law. Cush, who was crying, gently bent down and placed the box in the river. Then, in my mind's eye, I could see the box falling through the water, swaying a little as it went, until it hit the bottom, and little, dark grey clouds poofed out through the holes and dissipated into the water.

That was it. The men poled the barge a little way to a dock. Without saying anything or making eye contact, I just stood up and went down the gangway, and left. Marcella was on the opposite shore, where she'd watched the whole thing. Cornelius had decided to follow the Roman way and burn the bodies; he'd had enough of the ways of Jews and Christoi, who buried theirs. So, because of this, Marcella didn't feel she could participate, but did want to be present.

I walk through the Roman Quarter, by the old house. I try not to look, but I do. When I get to the arched stone bridge, there are soldiers there. They stop me, but I'm recognized as "the son-in-law of Lucius Cornelius. The soldier lets me pass but warns me that things are "still not settled over there." He waves to the soldiers on the other side of the bridge, and I pass.

Next thing, I'm in the courtyard of the school. Nothing's changed; no one's touched anything. There are still dead bodies strewn around; the thought surfaces that "Jews don't want to touch the dead," for purity's sake. I go to the well and take the pole with the rope and bucket out of its notch and off the support. I toss it over to one side, pull up the rope and bucket, and toss them, too. Then I try to dislodge the support, but it's planted too deeply or firmly in the ground. I can't budge it. I then approach one of the bodies; it's lying on its face. The whole place smells terrible, like badly spoiled milk only much stronger. The dead man has a knife in his back, just before half-way down his torso. I can see that it's very primitive, just a piece of metal that somebody affixed two thin pieces of wood to with two screws (or bolts?) for a handle. I reach down and pull it out; it comes out easily, with a feeling of being in something soggy. Ugggghhhh. The smell is awful. I wipe the blade on the dead person's robe, then I put it inside the folds of my

THE LAST ESSENE

clothes (on the right side). I then take the man by his ankles and (walking backwards) drag him to the well. His ankles feel all swollen and softer than they should. When I get to the well, I go up to his front and reach under his chest; I heft him up and over the stones (I don't turn him over; I don't want to see his face). The sound of him going down the well, is, I think, the most horrible sound I've ever heard; he clacks and bounces a little off the walls of the well, then hits the mucky ooze on the bottom with a "plop" sound and then the sound of being sucked down into it. But I just hurry to the next body and do the same thing; there must be 12–15 of them, all throughout the yard. I'm getting tired and wish that I'd started with the ones farthest away, so I that by the time I was near finishing, I'd have had the least distance to go.

When all the bodies are in the well, I go to the nearest quarters and begin taking old, burnt bricks, charred pieces of wood, etc., and dropping them down the well. I do this until it's almost filled to the top. Then I take the stones that make up the top of the well, and push them in. By the time it's done, there's a mound of stones, like a cairn, where the well used to be.

I sit down on the ground; I'm very tired. I reach into my clothing (on the left side) and pull out a folded-up piece of white cloth. I have a memory: It's the day Cush found me and brought me to my father-in-law. He'd already burnt the bodies, as he didn't feel he could wait in the heat, but he'd sent Cush to search for me. That night, I slept in La'nah's old room. There wasn't much left in it; most of her things had come to our place. I slept in her (very small) bed; it had a white sheet that still smelled like La'nah, like her hair. I almost couldn't stand it but didn't want to leave it. I thought of sleeping on the floor instead, but finally wrapped myself, head to toe, in the sheet like a dead person, and lay down in the bed. I smelled La'nah's smell around me all night. It was awful and comforting and not comforting, and I really didn't sleep. In the morning, the morning of the funeral, I folded the sheet very tight and slipped it into my clothes.

In the compound, I unlooped the top of the rope from the pole, pulled a measure of rope, then cut it with the knife (this wasn't easy; the rope was thick and the knife pretty dull). Then I took the rope, the folded sheet and the knife and left the school. When I came to the fountain in the square, I stripped off all my clothes. There was no one around; the square was abandoned, but I wouldn't have cared. I was dead already. I stepped into the lower basin of the fountain and washed that awful smell off me. When I got out, I took the sheet and folded it widthwise in half. Then I took the knife and cut a slit (more like "ripped," it was so dull) across the fold about eight inches, with a little slit perpendicular to it. Then I slipped the sheet over my head and put my head through the slit. I used the rope as a belt; the sheet was long enough to overlap a little on my sides. I left the old clothes right there, and the knife. I was done with the Essenes; I was never really one anyway. Then I walked back to the school.

There comes a time, even in past-life regression, when one needs to put away one's past. Apparently that time had arrived for Yossi. The theory also states that one is led in regression to the past-life memories most needed for one's present life.

THE LAST ESSENE

After the funeral of his La'nah and her mother, Yossi returns to the charred ruins of the Academy. The abandoned well with its Ooze where Yossi had hidden and saved himself will now serve another purpose. All of the dead will be disposed of there (in a rather unceremonious fashion). Over this Yossi raises a cairn of stones, one of the traditional forms of marking burial in the ancient world.

The meaning here is clear, I think. One part, a very major part, of Yossi's life has ended. He will be transitioning into something, but at this point he has no idea what that might be. Neither, it would seem, is he thinking about a future or seeking a direction. He is merely *being*, in that moment of ending, unvarnished and entirely present.

For me in the here and now, endings were also being allowed to occur, courtesy of my regression. I was seeing that Wayne-Daniel, Catholic Franciscan seminarian, although always a part of my past, was just that—my past. In my love for and relationship with Christine, I had come to move beyond the narrowness, the one-sidedness that had marked my formation in that culture. The union, the balance of Heart and Mind, of Feminine and Masculine, had taken firm root and would continue to grow.

I could see now the past-life trauma responsible for the phenomenon I'd called The Ooze. Having finally stopped "thinking beyond his heart," having fully embraced La'nah and with her all she represented, Yossi had had it all suddenly ripped away from him. I came to quickly realize that my fear, bordering on certainty, that Christine would somehow be ripped away from me as well, and that the cause of this would be a basic incompatibility between any advanced spiritual life and committed romantic love, was rooted here. I was largely reliving a past-life trauma. Sylvia's reminders that "this is now," her pointing out that, now that I knew the root of this distress, I could leave it in the past where it righty belonged, worked miracles. I never experienced the Ooze again.

The realization also grew that Yossi had not lost his Great Love because he was too spiritual to have one. Rather, La'nah's terrible death was the result of others not being spiritual *enough*. Yossi's attempts to open the minds and hearts of students to ideas beyond their own spiritual borders had made the Academy a target for the violently narrow-minded and those existentially threatened by concepts different from their own. La'nah's death was not a matter of a Divine righting of Yossi's course; it was a great wrong, a senseless crime against both the Head and the Heart.

It is interesting that all this took place in Egypt. In my studies with Rabbi Alan, I had come to learn that the Biblical Hebrew name for Egypt was *Mitzraim,* literally "Narrow Straits." Geographically this made sense, considering the centrality of the Nile and its branching off into a delta of near-infinite channels. Speaking spiritually, however, to be in Narrow Straits meant something very different! It was a state of tunnel vision, of closed-mindedness and hyper-focus on only one restrictive slice of reality. As God's name is I Will Be *Whatever* I Will Be, Narrow Straits is the opposite of God's reality. No wonder the ancient Hebrews needed to be freed from slavery to that place in order to know Revelation and to enter into the Land of the Promise!

Yossi's and my fear that to be truly close to God meant to be close to no one else was a prime example of slavery to Narrow Straits. My past-life regression experience was liberating me from that bondage.

Yossi, it would seem, was still very much in process. He cast off his Essenic clothing, and instead made himself a new overgarment of a sheet from La'nah's room. The slit through which he would push his head he cut with a primitive knife he'd taken from the body of one of the riot's Academy victims. Likewise, his belt was a length of rope from the abandoned well in which he'd hidden. He stripped naked right there in a public square and washed himself in its fountain.

The symbolism could not be more clear. Yossi had experienced a death and was coming back to life in a new way. He was no longer an Essene and realized he had not been for quite some time. His new robe, rope-belt, and knife would be constant reminders of this, agents of transition from one life to another. But what life?

Where would Yossi go now? What would he do? How could he possibly learn these things? How can near total loss—of home, of loving partner, of mission, of one's very identity—become a Land of Promise?

WAYNE-DANIEL BERARD

In his stunning verse play, *JB*, retelling the story of Job, the poet Archibald MacLeish writes,

"To be, become, and end are beautiful."

In very real ways, the life of Yossi as the last Essene had ended. I had come to see that same was true of Wayne-Daniel, as one of the last Franciscan minor seminarians. Who would we then be? What would we become? Could it be beautiful?

CHAPTER 15
Journeys Ended, Journeys Begun

I'd decided to "sit the seven days" for La'nah and her mother. I went into my old quarters. The front wall was still standing but the door was gone, and there was rubble piled up inside it. The roof had burnt and collapsed, leaning in on the right side like a lean-to. I went into that space; my old bed was in it, all charred. I decided to just sit here. That's what I did; I sat and let everything roll by me—the original Place, the fire, the desert, Amah, Ruth, everything. I didn't think about them, really; I just let them be there in front of me and then just roll by. I'd go out during the day to the fountain to drink (I never went out at night). I didn't eat anything. (There was a big rip in the side wall of my quarters, and I'd go through into the next one to go to the bathroom). I didn't go out to pray with the sun anymore, but I could see the moon through the slanted beams (like in a sukkah). I really liked the moon; it would get bigger and smaller and sometimes disappear altogether. I thought it was a much better symbol than the sun for how things really were.

When it got dark on the seventh day of the sitting, I decided I'd just leave. I didn't know where I was going; I'd decided to definitely not *go south and seek out Essenes. I was thinking that maybe I'd retrace my steps, back toward and into Israel, but I didn't really know. I stepped out of what was left of my quarters and couldn't believe what I saw. There was a semi-circle of people formed in front of my quarters. There was Yodi, sitting cross-legged; then Pote stood, beside him was Yoachanan, then the two Pythagorean women, then Marcella, and Cush. They each had a candle in some sort of gourd beside them on the ground. I asked them what they were doing there, and Pote said that they were "keeping the nights" with me. Apparently, they'd been there all seven nights, but I only went out to the fountain during the day. I asked how they'd survived the riots. Pote said that he'd been in the Egyptian Quarter that night, visiting people and couldn't get back. Marcella hadn't been at the villa; it hadn't been her turn to stay with La'nah. Still, the synagogue I'd visited had been burnt down. Yodi said, "I was here all the time." I asked how, and he said that when he saw the rioters crossing the yard, he'd lain down in front of his quarters, spread his orange robe over himself, flattened himself out and controlled his breathing. "They thought I was just a mound of cloth," he said, and although he'd been stepped on and kicked, he'd survived, and just waited until things died down, then escaped outside the walls and hid out anywhere he could. I asked about Philotides; Pote said he had been "in the library on the island," when he heard about the trouble. He insisted on taking a boat back and on trying to get to the school, even though people tried to talk him out of this. He was attacked by a mob and killed.*

I was extremely moved that these people would come here night after night for me. I thought to myself, "They really do love me." Then Pote asked what I was going to do next. I told him that I was just going to walk, that I didn't really care where I ended up. He nodded and said, "We go with you." (Actually, I could hear it very plainly in whatever language he was speaking. It sounded like "Sha'ah nah tuvah"). I couldn't believe it! I looked around at them; they were serious. Pote repeated it: "We go with you." Well, I couldn't very well make all these people just wander around with me! I asked him what his plans would be otherwise. He said that already the governor was talking about a grand rebuilding of the city, that he actually saw this as his big chance to do so. He would use the captured rioters as slaves. Pote felt sure that he would want to rebuild the school, especially with my connection to his chief aide. "But," he said, "we're each ready to go with you now, wherever you go." I hesitated for a minute; how could I ask these wonderful, caring people to give up on the school? So, I said, "Alright, I'll stay. But I can't say for how long." Pote moved toward me; I thought maybe he was going to embrace me. But he walked by me, up to my ruined quarters, and took a charred piece of wood out of the mess. Then he came back and stood in front of me; he put his left hand on my right shoulder, and with his right he traced the letter "Tau" on the front of my clothes. Then he took the stick and did the same thing to the front of his own robe. He walked back to his place in the half-circle and handed the stick to Yodi, who also traced a Tau on the front of his orange robe. Then the stick was passed from one to another; each did the same thing. We just stood there for a few seconds; I was so overwhelmed. Then Pote motioned for me to follow, and we all walked back through the broken gate. Pote and I turned left, toward the Egyptian Quarter.

The scene flashed forward: The yard was filled with men working and piles of clay bricks. I would come, but couldn't stand to just watch the slaves work; I'd join in with the carrying and placing of bricks. Fast forward a bit more: I'm walking down the new colonnade of the new academy (the colonnade now stretches all along all four walls, not just the front wall like before). The support by the mound of stones that had been the old well looks different. Someone put a wedge of wood in the "vee" of the support and added a cross bar over it, with two wedges attached, hanging down from the ends of the cross bar. Now the support looked like a letter "Tau"; that is apparently how the school is now called. I'm walking down the colonnade with Marcella and Cush (she's inside the academy now??) I feel okay. It's sad, but there's goodness, too. There's a peacefulness, even in the hurt.

For those not familiar with it, "to sit the seven days" is to engage in a Jewish mourning process called "shiva." This is very different from the perhaps better-known event of a wake. In Jewish life, a body is buried within twenty-four hours (if possible). Those who wish to pay their respects and to offer support for the family join them in their home for shiva. During this period, the bereaved are rarely left unattended. All household chores are done by supportive friends and family; people bring food—*lots* of food! Stories and memories are shared about the person who has died. Prayer services dot the week—all in the family's home.

Yossi decides to sit shiva for La'nah, her mother, and all whom he has lost in the violence. But for him, this is a solitary, meditative experience. He needs the solitude, the quiet, the time just to sit with all that has happened to him, without discussion or even condolence. Yossi chooses the bunt-out ruin of his old quarters for this experience.

It would seem that Yossi is doing far more than mourning his Great Love here. He is bearing witness to and wordlessly processing the end of the life he had known, the person he had been. In a way, he is sitting his own shiva—not so much mourning the passing of the last Essene as marking it fully and wishing to learn all he has experienced. He himself seems to recognize the necessity of this.

As my dear friends, the monks of Weston Priory sing,

Journeys ended, journeys begun:
to go where we have never been,
to be beyond our past . . .

Yossi's shiva lasts seven days, evoking echoes of the first week of Creation. When Yossi emerges from this time, his idea is to merely walk, without specific plan of purpose.

The Master doesn't seek fulfillment.
Not seeking, not expecting,
they are present, and can welcome all things.

—Lao Tzu

What Yossi did not expect he encounters in the moonlight of that seventh day. As he emerges from the ruins of his old life, he finds companions of the heart waiting for him. Yodi the Buddhist

Master, Pote, Yoachanan, Cush, the two Pythagorean woman, and Marcella had all been keeping vigil, all those seven nights.

Yossi is overwhelmed; love had not left him with the death of La'nah. He is deeply cherished and tendered by dear ones across the distinctions meant to divide us.

This is the opposite of abandonment.

When Pote asks him what he is now planning to do, Yossi speaks of his decision to "just walk." Pote insists that all of them would accompany him.

This particular past-life memory remains extremely strong with me. I had already identified Pote as my dear friend and spiritual mentor, Phi Anderson. I had likewise come to see the Pythagoreans women as two close friends of mine in my Jewish life, both amazing spiritual leaders in their communities. Although I have yet to see or recognize Yodi in this life, Cush I do realize as someone who had been very close to Christine's family. Yoachanan I had come to see as an old friend from my seminary days. I have already mentioned Reb Ishmael/Elisha as Rabbi Alan, and Avel as my dear friend and brother, Bill.

Yossi and I, both orphans, had known the disappointment or absence of family. This had in many ways shaped our lives, and not to the positive. Now, Yossi was experiencing true family, the family who chooses you and whom you choose, regardless of DNA connection. I, too, had and continue to experience this in the dear ones who have maintained with me the vigil of my life, and who would insist on companioning me through all the careening twists, the soaring flights and perilous plunges—through divorce and remarriage, through journeys ended and begun with faith traditions—saying always, "We go with you."

These are the people who put the "Om" in community.

The community surrounding Yossi is sealed by the tracing of the multi-meaninged Tau on the robes of each one present, drawn from the charred remains of what no longer was. But the Academy was not lifeless; violent intolerance may have won the day, but it would not necessarily win the next, and the next. Just as with the monks' song, there was another verse to sing,

. . . moments of lifting up,

transcending death,

rising in transparent life . . .

The Academy was being rebuilt—and a woman was now a full-fledged member! In my present life, a new president of my college would see fit to dissolve the Office of Chaplain—but my role as spiritual teacher and guide seemed to skyrocket exponentially, with courses like *The Spiritual Quest* and *Why (,) God?*, twice-weekly meditation sessions which needed to find a larger space, and energy-centered retreats for students, faculty, and staff at a nearby Buddhist temple.

In Hebrew, the equivalent of Tau is the letter Tav. It is, altogether fittingly, the letter that begins the phrases (in Hebrew), "You shall die" and "You shall live." Tav is both of them.

So now was Yossi. And so was I.

CHAPTER 16

Lekha Dodi

Session 10

It seemed to take some time to get back into the past life on this session (although I didn't realize until later how long. Christine said it was about 15 minutes, when I'd have estimated about 5–7). Sylvia needed to "count me down" a second time. I feel that this was most likely due to the three-week lay off since the last session.

I did begin to see pyramidic shapes (a recurring image) on the "dark screen" of my closed eyes. Soon things filled in. These were smaller pyramids, three or four of them, on the other side of a canal, in the general area where I and the others went to pray each morning. I immediately knew that Pote had died. I felt a real sense of loss; I missed him very deeply. At the same time, there was a feeling that this was part of the flow of things and that even the missing of him had its place in my life.

WAYNE-DANIEL BERARD

The scene shifted, and I was walking under the new colonnade with Marcella and Cush. Those at the school had wanted me to assume leadership after Pote's death, but I'd declined. Rather, we now all make decisions together. In Philotides' old quarters there is a big table, shaped like an oval with the little ends flattened. We all sit around this, but leave the two ends empty, for Philotides and Pote; it also shows that no single person is the leader. The two Pythagorean women and Marcella have a seat at the table, as does Cush (who is in charge of all the buildings and the property). The women do not teach male students, but beyond that they are equal members of the place.

I can tell that Marcella has an interest in me. But I also have no sense inside of wanting to have a relationship again. I feel that "I'm done with all this." My insides still reverberate with all that happened with La'nah and with the loss of her. I just have none of that sort of energy.

All the quarters have been rebuilt, except, at my request, my old one. I asked that it be left as it was, except to clean out the rubble, so no vermin would take up residence. I don't live there myself, but across the compound in new quarters. But I wanted to memorialize what had happened and the people who died. At the same time, occasionally someone will come to the school looking for answers, not just for learning, but because they are in great pain. They seem to come to me. I ask them to sit the seven days, to mourn whatever it is that's causing them hurt. We use my old quarters. For part of it I may sit with them and leave them alone for others. I may teach them the breathing that Yodi taught me. I see myself bringing a basket of flat bread with a course white cloth over it and an earthenware jug to the door. At night, I sit out by the door with a candle in a little gourd and keep

THE LAST ESSENE

vigil (although sometimes I stretch out with a blanket and sleep there, too!).

There is one young man; he seems to be Roman by his clothing and his hair. He has lost his mother; his father is distant. So, we do what I described above. At the end of day seven, he comes out of the burnt-out quarters. He thanks me with much feeling and says he's going. I ask him where he will go, and he responds, "Home to my father. I'll try to tell him about all this." I say, "I'll go with you, if you want." The boy seems stunned. He thanks me but says no. I answer, "Well, even if I don't go with you, I'll go with you." I take a burnt-out stick from the ruin and make the "Tau" on the front of his toga. He bows very deeply, and so do I. Then I watch him walk across the compound and out the gate.

It seems that this happens more and more. People with grief come, and I sit with them like this. Soon, I'm not doing much teaching anymore, but more and more of this. There is something very deep and right-feeling about it.

At dawn, I still go to the same place to pray toward the sun. The others do so, too. Cush and Marcella say their prayers to the Christos (she now always stands next to me in Pote's old place). Yoachanon also prays, with his tallit and phylacteries. The two Pythagorean women are there. The smaller one has an instrument, like a simple harp, only three or four strings, stretched on crossed sticks, down to what looks like a large turtle shell. She just strikes a chord and the sound lingers; that's all they do—one chord, some stillness, then another. Yodi sits in his lotus position—no blanket, how does he do that in the hot sand? We do this every morning.

Yossi continues what can be described as the "liberalization" of the Academy. Women and a former servant now share equally in the decision making. (I have come to see that the term "Cush" refers to a nation and people south of Egypt, sometimes also spelled "Kush." This would make sense, as Cush is a Black man).

The most interesting thing about this regression for me involves Yossi's reaction to Marcella, or lack thereof. He is getting the strong impression that she is interested in him romantically. For him, this is way too soon after the loss of La'nah. But he also seems to feel that he is "done with all this," that is, that he will never experience such love again. Or is it that he will never allow himself to?

Such feelings are not unusual for anyone who has lost their Great Love. For me, the interesting question is: Will such feelings continue? Will Yossi ever permit himself to be open to love again. Would I in this life, were it Christine who was lost?

Complicating this was my present life recognition of Marcella. Mention has already been made of a woman for whom I had very strong feelings as my first marriage was ending but before I had come to know Christine. Let us call her "Aidi" (the first entry in

THE LAST ESSENE

an online list of girls' names. It means "Beginning" in French). Although Aidi expressed strong feelings for me as well, she was also involved with someone else. In the end, she chose him. Although this was incredibly painful at the time, I did accept it, and later was just as incredibly thankful for it. Aidi was not my Great Love, although this opening to love did in many ways make my relationship with Christine possible.

Later I would come to see the karma of the situation being played out here. As Yossi, I had rejected Marcella's overtures; as Aidi, she would reject mine. A karmic balance was restored, and the realization of best possible outcomes allowed to materialize.

But what about Yossi and love, post-La'nah? Was he truly "done with all that?" Would he never love again? Would I, if (please, God, no!) anything ever happened to Christine?

In my present life, I did experience a scare of just this sort. A physical exam revealed the existence of a possible heart problem for Christine. As it turned out later, the test had been inaccurate; nothing was wrong. But before that came to be known, I went into a panic! I hovered over Christine, constantly urging her about diet, exercise, etc. It soon became apparent that, if I kept it up, there would indeed be a death—Christine was going to kill me! She recommended, and I concurred, that I should take my feelings to Eve, my therapist.

I spoke at length with Eve about this, insisting that if were to lose Christine, I would want to "throw myself off a bridge." Eve suggested applying a technique to this situation called EMDR, Eye Movement Desensitization and Reprocessing. Without going into detail, this technique helps one to move past blocks that can prevent us from dealing with great pain.

Using this process, Eve asked me to place myself into the feeling of panic about Christine's situation, to imagine myself, for instance, back in the place where she first told me of her initial diagnosis. When I did this, freed from the barriers to experiencing the full brunt of my feelings, I was nearly drowned in intense fear, sorrow, and hopelessness. But something else, something completely unexpected, happened as well.

Behind my closed eyes, I found myself back in time, to the fall of 1967, to be exact. I was then a sophomore in minor seminary, and, quite literally, at the edge of the precipice. My experience of Franciscan life had been one of rejection and isolation. I'd soon come to see that there was little place for someone truly seeking the loving, compassionate reality of God in formal seminary. The overt uber-masculinity of the Church and its training ground left anything of that sort worthy only of scorn and derision—and anyone identified with it as outcast completely. I had never felt so alone as I did in "God's academy."

The only place worse was my home neighborhood and its schools; at least in seminary no one beat you, leaving you unconscious in the street or schoolyard (as had happened to me on more than one occasion).

So where was I to go? The only way was down.

There in Eve's office, I relived that night when, at fifteen, I put my winter coat over my pajamas, tied my sneakers, and snuck off the grounds toward the nearby bridge over the Delaware River. Once there, I slung my right leg over the steel tubing of the rail and prepared to escape my suffering.

Sitting with Eve, I recognized the same feelings erupting in memory as I'd felt about Christine's potential loss: hopelessness, despair, utter loneliness, and emptiness. My memory replayed my leaning over the edge . . .

Then it happened. A sense, a feeling—of an arm wrapping itself across my right shoulder, holding me back.

I shuddered, on the bridge as well as right there in the office. What was this?

Under EMDR, I remembered trying once more to pull myself over the railing. Again, that arm, that restraint. But this time, a voice reverberated inside me. I did not so much hear it as felt it, its intention, its message. As if the voice was somehow able to bypass the ears and deliver its meaning right to the heart.

"*Don't do this to us,*" the Voice said.

And that Voice was Feminine.

I remembered pulling myself back, vigorously shaking my head. Was I losing my mind? And yet the reverberation of that Voice still resonated inside of me, like the remnants of a bell tolling, a bell that was my entire being.

I turned around and walked back up the hill to the seminary and returned to bed. I told no one anything about this.

"What do you think that Voice was?" Eve asked me. "Whose was it?"

"I think it was Shekinah," I replied with no filters there to prevent me. "The Divine Feminine."

I was familiar with the idea of God's Feminine and Masculine Sides. In Judaism, that Divine Feminine had a name, *Shekinah*. It meant "Indwelling Presence." The Divine Masculine was seen as

THE LAST ESSENE

somewhat aloof and regal. Distant. Shekinah dwelt within, in intimacy with us.

Shekinah, the Divine Feminine, was exactly what had been missing in the seminary and in the Church in general. She seemed entirely absent from Yossi's Essenic experience, as well—the concept would not truly emerge until the writing of Talmud, barely begun in Yossi's day; in fact, he would help to write some of it!

But why had this memory emerged, in a psychotherapeutic session about panic over my wife's health?

The answer was relatively simple: Christine was the manifestation of Shekinah in my present life, just as La'nah had been Her manifestation in Yossi's. Shekinah was the other half, the missing complimentary to the God that had been all-encompassing in both my and Yossi's earlier life. To lose Christine, to lose La'nah, would seem like losing God, or that manifestation of God that had finally squared the circle and made us both whole.

So, where did that leave us?

I emerged from this session, blurry-eyed and filterless (warning: do not drive after EMDR!), to find that there was much more to Christine than just Christine, that as a manifestation of the Divine Feminine in my life, she was limitless and unlosable. If anything were to happen to her, yes, I would be devastated but I would not "throw myself off a bridge"—been there, not been allowed to do that! Rather, whether that Loving Presence manifested itself in a new relationship or in any other form of Shekinah-ness, I would be ready and open.

Much the same, I think, could be said for Yossi. His response to those seeking him out because they were in pain seems be one and the same as his love for La'nah and his experience of the Divine Feminine through their love. Although the Tau Academy is an academic institution, Yossi welcomes the Roman young man, sits with him, and even offers to accompany him on his journey to his father, literally and symbolically. The Head and Heart, the Divine Masculine and Divine Feminine have become one.

I believe that Yossi, without being able to identify it by name, was growing in the realization of Shekinah. Even without La'nah, his future belonged to Love.

> Shekinah
> is pregnant
> with my
> future,
>   she smiles
> at me
> from our
> blue mat,

THE LAST ESSENE

round as
the curve
of whisper
across the
pillow,
she places
my hand
"there," she
says nothing kicks,
no elbows, but
an astrolabe
ripples and
arcs across
my next day,
and my next,
and next to me
she presses
my cheek to
tomorrow
"yedid," she
whispers
I hum *lekha
dodi* resonate

    Together.

(Hebrew – *Yedid*: Beloved. *Lekhu dodi*: "Come, Beloved," sung to welcome Shabbat)

CHAPTER 17

Right Action

The scene shifts: I'm in my new quarters, and there's a knock. It's Cush (who's very short; I can see all of him in the small doorway). There's a man outside with a message. The man looks like a Bedouin; his head and face are almost all covered. He hands me what looks like a wooden tube about an inch and half in diameter. Each end is covered with a thick red wax. I take it inside with Cush and open it by pushing my thumb through the wax (which is surprisingly not easy!). There's a little scroll inside with a message; it's from another Torah academy in "the province of Asia." It is in a town or city called "Nisbis" or "Nisibis." (The scroll is written in Greek characters. It's hard to always make writing out in these regressions. As Yossi, there's the voice in "my" head reading in Greek, which isn't my first language—and which my present self doesn't understand at all. Then I "hear" it or sense it in English, so it's twice removed). Those at this Academy are writing and compiling thoughts on the Torah; they know that I was the disciple of Rabbi Ishmael and am also a scholar. Would I come and join in the work? I tell Cush I will have to think about it, but inside I already know I'm going. I just feel that I'm done here and that it's time.

THE LAST ESSENE

Next I see the big table in Philotides' old quarters. We each have a turn to speak—there are many newer faces, newer members that I don't know well. I tell them of the invitation and my decision. No one tries to talk me out of it. Cush, who sits to my left, says, "I am coming." I tell him that he doesn't have to do this. He just keeps looking straight ahead and says, "I am coming." So that's that!

When it comes to Marcella's turn, she announces that she, too, is leaving. She's been asked to come to Cyprus to settle dispute among the Christoi there. She says that things are getting more difficult in the city. Two camps, one of Jewish Christoi and one of non-Jewish, expect people to make a choice. She says that her father's message is being lost. She also says we could travel together when we leave.

I don't want to walk on this journey; I've had enough of all the walking. We take a boat, she, Cush and me. Next, I'm sitting on a plank bench along the side of a rather small boat. We're not really out to sea but following the coast. Still, this is the ocean, and I'm not used to the up and down. I feel I may get sick, and don't want to do so in front of Marcella who's sitting beside me (but not very close, thankfully). Cush is nowhere to be seen—thanks so much for leaving me alone with her! I think he's enjoying this.

We get to a port in Cyprus; Marcella is about to go down the gangplank. She says that I could stop here on my return. But I know inside I'm not going to return. I thank her and say, "May the peace of your Christos be with you." Then she turns and walks down the gangway. To my surprise, I feel a sense of loss as she walks away. But

WAYNE-DANIEL BERARD

I can't bring myself to call after her or to do anything about it. My insides are just too battered.

Then the scene shifts: I'm in the new Academy. It's very Greek looking; white walls, classical columns and colonnade. I'm walking beside a man who appears to be very old. He's a very small man and all bent over; he supports himself with a stick with two curved pieces coming from its top, forming a sort of handle. His tunic is greenish blue. I understand that he's Jewish, but he has long white hair, brushed back, and a receding hairline. He doesn't look up as he walks. I'm on his left, and although I don't support him, I'm very conscious of watching out for him. It feels that I've been at the new Academy only a few days. As we walk (actually, he hobbles) down the colonnade, he's speaking with me. He says that more violence and war is coming, and that we must preserve all that we can beforehand. I call him "Abba," and already feel a great deal of affection for him, like for a grandfather. He has an air about him, like someone who has great intellectual knowledge but also a great heart. I really like him. His name is Yaakov (Jacob), and he is called "Jacob the Translator," because he translates Hebrew and Aramaic texts to Greek and vice-versa. He says that he knew my master and that he was a great man. I ask, "Why did you send for me, Abba?" He stops and has to crane his chin up to look at me. He has one of those faces with almost no chin; his cheeks are kind of sunken (like when elderly people don't wear their dentures). An odd thing is that he has no face hair except for his eyebrows; there's no stubble or little strands. It looks like he doesn't have a beard at all. And his eyes are very striking, kind of a grey blue. He says, "Aren't you the one that sits with people who have hurt in their hearts?" I say, "Yes, Abba." He then says, "The heart of the Torah is hurting, the heart of the people is hurting." He stops and says, "If I had only known you earlier, my life would have turned out so much differently." Then he looks down again, and we continue to walk. I really love this beautiful old man. I'm glad I'm here.

Next I am going up the white marble steps to the hall of the Academy. Inside there are amphitheater-like benches, also made of stone, where the discussion and debate over Torah and the commentary being written takes place. I get to the vestibule and stop. I don't want to do this; I don't want to join in debate anymore. I then see myself back in my new room, writing out something on a piece of parchment (with a white quill). Abba Jacob has told me that I don't have to attend the meetings; I can just write out my thoughts on the passage in question, and he will deliver it to the assembly. Nice.

One thing I notice toward the end of the session: I begin to itch. In the past life, Yossi sees that he has tear-drop shaped bumps here and there on his face and arms. I'm sitting on the steps in front of my new quarters, scratching, saying to myself that I should "speak with someone" about them. (In the chair, I'm scratching myself).

At this point, Sylvia began to bring me out of the regression.

This session was considerably less difficult emotionally than the two previous ones, even though it took more time to get started. It was interesting that things seemed to be a bit more "compressed" (for lack of a better term); it seemed that the regression wasn't stopping for as much detail as it often had. Also, I seemed to come in and out of "being Yossi" and being an observer, much more than in previous sessions.

WAYNE-DANIEL BERARD

I feel strongly that I should recognize Jacob from my present life, but nothing's coming.

Do you have the patience to wait
till your mud settles and the water is clear?
Can you remain unmoving
till the right action arises of itself?

— Lao Tzu

Yossi, it seems, had been doing exactly what the *Tao Te Ching* would have recommended to him. He simply waited, in readiness.

When the invitation arises to engage in what will become, at least in part, the creation of Talmud, the second most sacred set of writings in Judaism (after Torah), Yossi is ready.

Sylvia had long before given me the green light to research whatever presented itself in our sessions. Nisibis (today, Nusaybin) was a town in modern-day Turkey, then the Roman province of Asia. It sits on the border with Syria. I had never in my life heard of this place, nor did I know that the town had been a center of Jewish learning during the 2nd century (exactly the time of Yossi) attracting students from great distances. The invitation

THE LAST ESSENE

to join in this work came *specifically* because Yossi had been a disciple of Reb Ishmael; this would indicate that a certain more progressive approach was being taken. Naturally, Yossi jumps at the chance to extend his old Master's work and at the validation the invitation seems to offer the Tau Academy. That, and it is clear that Yossi's time in Alexandria had run its course.

The one possible hitch is Marcella.

The daughter of John Mark is being called to the island of Cypress, to try to calm tensions there between Jews of the Jesus School of Judaism and other Jews. Historically, we know that such was the case; The Pharisee Movement had emerged from the ruins of the Great Revolt to assume (with Roman approval) the leadership of what was left of Jewish life. The Pharisees felt strongly that in order to survive, Judaism needed to speak with only one voice—theirs. Other forms of Judaism were being pushed out; pluralism in Jewish life was fast becoming a thing of the past.

Was it an accident that Yossi and Marcella travelled north together in the same boat? In regression, I had the very strong sense that the answer was no. Marcella had developed strong feelings for Yossi and would have dearly loved for them to be returned, and for the former Essene to join her in her work—and more! As Marcella disembarks the ship, Yossi does experience a twinge of regret, but feels certain that his "insides are just too battered" to explore romantic relationship at this point. Besides, he has had all the drama, all the religious debate and conflict he can endure for one lifetime.

Interestingly enough, it seems that it is the Heart, even more than the Head, which has led to Yossi's presence in Nisibis. Although his new Master, Jacob the Translator, expresses admiration for Reb Ishmael, he seems much more interested in Yossi's reputation for "sitting with someone who had hurt in their heart." Yossi, for his part, acknowledges feeling real affection for this elderly scholar—feelings he seems to acknowledge and accept much more readily since La'nah. (I can never recall him admitting such feelings for Avel, Ismael, Amma, Ruth, Pote, or anyone other than La'nah).

Endearing him further to Yossi is Jacob's willingness to allow him to forego the oftentimes rancorous debate in the Academy. One can only imagine, what with his experiences of near escape with Ishmael and the destruction and death caused by the Alexandrian riots, how triggered such an atmosphere would leave Yossi.

Sitting in regression, I almost but not quite recognize this kind elder as someone from my present life. I feel sure that the "right recognition" will eventually arise of itself.

CHAPTER 18

The One True Faith

Past-Life Regression
Session 11

It took a shorter period of time for something to "materialize" in my field of vision than in the last session. But it took a moment or two to recognize what it was. It turned out to be a face, but one in very close proximity to my own, so it was blurry and distorted. I soon realized that I (Yossi) was lying down on the ground outside; I couldn't move anything but my eyes. The face was hovering just an inch or two above mine, seemingly checking me out.

Then the scene shifted. I knew I was looking at something from several weeks previous. I was sitting outside my quarters in the new Academy (very Greek looking with classical colonnade). It was night with a big moon; it was sort of a mix of warm and cool outside. I was itchy from the little eruptions on my skin. For a moment, I was observing this *from the outside, then it shifted to where I was Yossi, experiencing everything. At that point, I heard a "click, click, click," very rhythmic and coming closer. I looked back over my shoulder down the colonnade to my right, and saw Reb Jacob coming along; the "click" was the sound of his stick on the colonnade floor. He stopped just short of behind me and said that bathing in the river (nearby) was good for sores, that the river was known for its medicinal properties. I knew this river, as I would go to a spot on its bank every dawn to pray. I thanked him and said that I would try it. He replied that he used to enjoy going to the river when he had been better able to get around. I said, "Would you like to go to the river, Abba? I could take you." He just peered his head around at me (he is very hunched over and can't seem to straighten up) and said, "Good." Then he "clicked" away down the colonnade.*

The scene then shifted; it was the next morning. I was standing in the courtyard; the Abba was there and so were four or five other men, other scholars in the Academy, younger than he, but older than me. (I would estimate my age by my appearance to be in my late 20s?). I said, "Are you ready, Abba?" He nodded. So, I bent and picked him up in my arms like a baby. I could hear the shock of the others, their quick intake of breath. Cush opened the gate, and we walked out.

Abba Jacob wasn't very heavy, but after a while I did want to shift him. I said so, and put him up on my shoulders, like carrying a child. I got the distinct sense he was enjoying this; he didn't see "up" often anymore due to the curvature of his spine. In my right hand I held his right, along with my stick with the brass Tau on top; in my left, I held his left hand, with his stick dangling from it. He was so hunched over that I could almost feel his chin on the top of my head.

THE LAST ESSENE

We got to a spot by the river where there's a little bend; there were palm trees and shorter, beach grass. Over to our right was taller, marshy grass. I wanted to put Abba down, but realized that he probably couldn't sit up for long without some support. So, I took his stick, which had a double-curved handle, and propped its tip in the sand behind him; the other end he leaned back upon. Then I took off my clothes, leaving on only the girded cloth I wore underneath, and went into the river.

It was cold! I waded out to about my stomach, then dipped myself in three times, like in a mikvah. When I came out, Abba said, "I haven't been in a mikvah in years." I asked if he would like to go in, then picked him up again, baby-style. I waded back in with him (he kept his clothes on; they were a bluish purple). I asked if he wanted to be dipped, and he nodded. So, in three times we went. Again, he seemed to be enjoying himself!

When we got back to the shore, we didn't have any towels. So, we sat and waited to dry off in the sun, which was rising higher and hotter. We sat back to back, so that I could support him. His head barely made it up to my upper back.

We sat for a few minutes saying nothing; the sun was very warm. Then he said, "I have something to tell you, Yossi. But I don't think you'll want anything more to do with me after you hear it." I said, "Never, Abba, never." He paused a second or two, then told me that he had been a scholar even as a very young man, that later he and

Reb Akiva had studied together and been friends. "After the war" he had become one of Yohanan's party (the Pharisee leader), who believed that the Jewish people "needed to speak with one voice," and that anything but a very traditional approach was dangerous. When Yohanan recommended advising the Romans that the Assah were a threat, Yaakov and Akiva had agreed. Yaakov had wholeheartedly supported the action against the Assah—the action that had caused the burning of my first home. Now he regretted it; he couldn't believe that he had ever supported the shedding of Jewish blood. "Yossi," he said, "I sent out messengers; I looked everywhere for any remaining Assah. But I couldn't find any. Then I heard about you and invited you here. I'm responsible for so much harm. How can I ever be forgiven? I can't forgive myself."

His voice was breaking, and I just felt so badly for this poor old man. I couldn't see him, as we were back to back. But I straightened up a little, lifted my arms a bit, and prayed out loud, "Oh Master of the universe, hear me. I am the last Assah. And in the name of all the Assahyim, we forgive Reb Yohanan. We forgive Reb Akiva. We forgive Reb Yaakov. We forgive even the Romans. And we ask you to forgive, as well, oh Lord. Let there be an end to all this; let there be no more hurt from this, Lord. Let it all be put aside forever." Then I leaned back with my right hand as far as I could, trying to reach Abba Jacob's hand. But I could only get as far as his upper wrist; it was so thin and bony, like a dog's arm. I held it and said, "There, Abba."

I could feel him crying; his breathing was uneven against my back. Then he said, "There is more. I had a son, my only son, my only child. I wanted him to be a great scholar, to repair the shame of our family. My grandfather, your old master, was considered a great heretic. His daughter was my mother. I never met him; I married as young as I could and had my son very young as well. I tried to train him myself, but he was no scholar. He was very kind and good-hearted; when he was a boy, if we squashed a bug, he would cry. But he had great trouble learning. Still, I worked him and worked him. When the time came for him to be a bar mitzvah, Akiva himself came to lead the ceremony. But when my son went to the bima, he began to stammer and shake. He couldn't go on. I was furious. I stood beside him and called him terrible things. I said he was an ox, a pig. That he was only fit to eat grass and garbage. That he had disgraced the family on purpose, just to injure me. That night, my son ran away. My wife was frantic, but I told her that he'd come home when he was tired and hungry. Actually, I didn't care if he ever did come back. I didn't even look for him at first. By the time I did, it was too late. We never saw him again. A few months later, my wife came down with "the half-alive sickness" (it took me a minute, in the chair, to decipher what he was saying here). Half her body went dead and she could no longer speak. A few months later, she was dead. But God punished me; not long after her death, I began to have this sickness. My spine began to bend worse than ever; my skin became like wax, and my beard fell out . . . it wasn't until years later, after the war, that I had any idea what had happened to my son. He had run off into the wilderness, and the Assah had found him. Apparently, he died . . . in the same attack which I myself had urged so strongly! *I did this.*" Then he cried a little, and said, "Maybe you knew of him, Yossi? His name was Avel."

"Avel?!" I said, "Avel?! I knew Avel! He was a great man, a good man. He was the Boys' Master. He was kind to us; he never struck us. When we'd have partial fasts, he'd sneak us a little food. He saved my life when the Romans came." And I told him the story of the attack, of my escape through the water grate. "You would have been proud of him," I said. When I finished the story, he asked, "Did he have you take a scroll with you?" I said, "No, Abba. He just said, 'Run Yossi, and keep on running. Save yourself.'" "Good," Abba said. "He was a better man than his father would have been."

I could feel Abba really weeping and shaking against my back now. He just kept saying, "My son, my only son. My son, my only son." I wanted to hold him, but we were back to back. So, I reached my arms around backwards and held him that way; he was so little and frail. And I said, "Not your only son, Abba. Not your only son." Then we just sat there, back to back. He cried and I cried.

After a while, I picked him back up, and we returned to the Academy. I called for someone to open the gate, and they did. As I came in with the Abba on my shoulders, I could see the others glaring at me; they were not at all happy.

At that point, images became a little more compressed. Sometimes I'd take Abba Jacob to the river with me; sometimes I'd go alone. My itch was improving. He and I would talk about the school in Egypt, about the different types of people teaching there, about the riots and La'nah. I had the sense this went on for several weeks.

I can recall in this and in the previous session wondering if Yossi had made any real progress at all in terms of spiritual institutional

THE LAST ESSENE

communities, such as the Essenes, The Alexandrian Academy, and now this academy in Nisibis. It seemed as if he kept being drawn back to such places, regardless of his past experience with them. Could I likewise see this playing out in my present life—first with my joining seminary, and then with being a part of several communities and enterprises, the latest being Jewish Renewal? What was Yossi truly looking for? What was I? Was it simply a case of, "That didn't work, let's try it again?" Was I caught in an unreconciled cycle of Yossi's making?

On several levels, I think I could understand all this. The boy I had been in the 1st century and in the 20th had both been orphans. Were Yossi and I primarily looking for home in these communities? Had Pote and Jacob (and to an extent, Avel, Ishmael, and Phil Anderson) been father figures to the same reborn soul across the stretches of time?

Then there was also the very real issue of maintaining a living. What career opportunities exist for a last Essene? And the chance to work on what would become Talmud? There could be reasons other than a search for home involved here for Yossi.

As the regression unfolded, a deeper reason seemed to emerge.

Abba Jacob was a man of intense, almost unbearable suffering. It became clear later that it was Yossi's reputation as someone who sits with those who have been "hurt in their hearts" that caused Jacob to call him in the first place. The two soon strike up a relationship. Someone who has known as much death and displacement as has Yossi will not be held back by the niceties of convention: if his friend wants to go to the river, Yossi will pick him up and carry him there. If he wishes to go into the water and perform the ritual bath (*mikveh*), Yossi will make that happen, as well. The good thing about having undergone death and rebirth is that old, petty restraints die with you—and stay dead.

At the river's edge, an amazing and poignant scene unfolds: the younger Yossi and the much older Yaakov, sitting back to back supporting each other in the warm sun, as Yaakov/Jacob unburns his tormented soul.

He feels that he had been a terrible father; he put his personal views on religion and scholarship about everything else, including his family (talk about Head and Heart!) In the process he had shamed and lost his own son. Beyond this, he had been part of the effort that convinced the Romans to destroy the center of Essenic life in Judea; he had been complicit in the chain of events that had cost the child Yossi the only home he had ever known. Later, he learned that his son had become an Essene and had died in that same attack—that son was Avel!

How would Yossi react?

There is a saying that "There is indeed one true faith—and it is called 'Forgiveness.'"

THE LAST ESSENE

Yossi's reaction to Jacob's revelation is to call out Yossi's forgiveness, as the last Essene, of Yaakov and all those responsible for that fateful attack. And more than this, he implores God to forgive them as well. He calls for "no more hurt from this," for it being "put aside forever."

Then Yossi takes an even further step into that one true faith. As Jacob laments the loss of his only son, Yossi assures him, "Not your only son, Abba." He is offering his own heart in sonship to a man (at least partially) responsible for one of the deepest pains of his life, and for the loss of Yossi's first caring father figure.

How had he come to this? How was such forgiveness possible?

Had Yossi forgotten entirely about personal responsibility? About justice?

Yes, he liked this man—but come on!

Had his experience with La'nah caused the heart to totally overwhelm the head?

I think that perhaps something quite different was happening here.

One of the pivotal, guiding sayings in my life is attributed to the great German writer, Goethe:

"I know of no act so terrible, that I cannot imagine myself, under the proper circumstances, committing it."

All throughout his life, Yossi had been surrounded, one might say besieged, by the opposite of that saying. The Essenes, for all their mysticism and kindness to the orphaned, were judgmental in the extreme, believing that they and they alone possessed the truth. Those at Reb Ishmael's academy were so incensed with his ideas that he was forced to flee for his life in the night. La'nah's life and the life of her baby were taken in just this sort of violent rejection of humility, of critical self-reflection. Those who lived this way, who committed such acts, were convinced that only they had the one true faith, and its name was anything but Forgiveness.

Yet it seems that Yossi had not joined them. Even in his incalculable loss, he had not expressed hatred for those inflicting it upon him or sought vengeance of any sort. Luckily, he had also had heart-companions on the way, ones with their own great gifts of intellect—Ishmael, Pote, Philotides, Yodi, and yes, Marcella, as well. They had every bit as much right to insist on the "one trueness" of their positions, and to act exactly as were the now powerful Pharisee party in terms of those who viewed things differently (as, unfortunately the faith growing from Marcella and her father's work would one day do). Instead, Yossi seems to have

THE LAST ESSENE

opened out, not closed off, in his work as a scholar of inclusiveness, *and* in his life as an ambassador of the heart.

And what of me? What of Yossi's reincarnation so many centuries into the future? What of my wounds, my grievances, my old resentments?

What could I imagine myself never doing, despite the circumstances, and therefore never truly forgiving?

CHAPTER 19

Last Lesson?

At that point, images became a little more compressed. Sometimes I'd take Abba Jacob to the river with me; sometimes I'd go alone. My itch was improving. He and I would talk about the school in Egypt, about the different types of people teaching there, about the riots and La'nah. I had the sense this went on for several weeks.

I have come to recognize who Reb Jacob is in my present life: brother (and Abbot) Leo, founder of Weston Priory in Vermont. Brother Leo was a pioneer in reforming monastic life, initiating decision-making by consensus and encouraging brothers in community to pursue and share their creative passions—from this came the beautiful songs that were earlier quoted here. Brother Leo was also a leader in the Ecumenical Movement, having been the primary author of Nostra Aestate, *the very progressive Vatican II document on the Church and the Jews.*

I knew brother Leo toward the end of his life. His energy was one of near transparent light. It was with great joy that I brought my friend

THE LAST ESSENE

and mentor, Phil Anderson, on a trip to Weston, whether he met brother Leo (Pote and Jacob meeting 1800 years later!). "I hope you come back" Leo said to Phil in parting; then he turned to me with an incisive twinkle in his eyes and said, "I know you will be back!"

Returning to that day's session: The scene had shifted. It was very early, and I was at the river alone; not even Cush was with me. When I came out of the cold water, I saw that my clothes were gone. "Wonderful!" I thought "Someone's playing a prank on me." I was going to have to walk back in my underwear. Then, thwack! I felt something hit my left upper arm. It was a rock! I turned in the direction it seemed to come from and thwack! Another rock hit me in the upper left of my chest. God, they were trying to stone me! I threw myself flat on the ground. Now more stones came, some landed around me, some on me.

*I was furious! I had had enough! Enough of attacks and burnings and mobs and running! I decided that I'd go right at them; they were hiding in the tall marsh grass. "At least," I said to myself, "I'll cut down the angle." So, I got up and roared, and started running toward the tall grass (my stick was likewise missing). The rocks were coming; I put my hand up over my face. Some were hitting, and it did hurt, but I was making headway. When I found them, I'd tear them apart! Then, all of a sudden—**BANG!** I felt this terrible impact at the back of my neck (remember when you'd bang your head as a child, and not feel any hurt at first, just the concussion?) Someone must have gotten around behind me. I felt an awful electric shock through my arms and legs. Then I fell on my back. I couldn't move my arms or legs, nothing but my eyes. I could still breathe. I remember thinking, "I'm paralyzed! What will happen now? Cush will come looking for me* eventually . . ." Then I saw that face leaning over me. He looked for a few seconds, then moved off. I saw sky. My breathing started to catch in my throat. Then it moved to just my nose. Then everything just dissolved, disappeared.

It was like when you wake up from a dream and suddenly everything is gone. Even the little squiggles and such that you see when you close your eyes weren't there. There were the dark pixels, but that was it. Sylvia asked me if the spirit had left the body, and I said yes. It felt like I was inside of things. It felt very, very soft. That was the word I kept using—"soft." Like this was what soft was, and then someone invented velvet, based on this. It was so peaceful, utterly relaxed. I loved it; I could have just stayed there forever.

At this point, Sylvia began bringing me out of the session.

I found this all very surprising, not at all what I'd expected. With those sores, I figured I (Yossi) would have some long, lingering illness. And I'd imagined that, when he did die, I might see "the blue tunnel, the light." But it wasn't at all like that; I didn't feel like I went anywhere, but rather everything else fell away. I did have a distinct sense of being "inside" of things, or rather, that I always had been, but now the "outside" had dissolved, like it was just an idea or a thought. I didn't hear or see any "Masters," as the Weiss books had spoken about, at least not so far.

I was also surprised, in retrospect, that I had rushed the people stoning me. After everything Yossi had been through, now he decides to fight *back? When I examine it, it seems he'd have had a much better chance just crawling into the river. But that thought never even crossed my (his) mind.*

CHAPTER 20

Oceans and Shot Glasses

I am so disappointed in Yossi.

After the last past-life memory, involving so much forgiveness on his part, I was ready to nominate Yossi for sainthood (had I still been Catholic). Now, what I feel concerning him is primarily letdown.

I certainly can understand his anger, given all he had gone through. And I realize he had moved beyond his Essenism, including (it would seem) its commitment to pacifism. But this?

On that riverbank, Yossi seemed to have turned his back on all that he had learned, all that this incarnation had taught him. Whereas at one time the Head had almost completely excluded the Heart, now it seemed that emotion possessed him totally, at least at that moment—so much so that he literally "couldn't think to save his own life." He did not consider going back into the river, perhaps to the other side (could Yossi swim?) It certainly would have not been the first time he had found himself alone in a wilderness, and he had survived. One could even say that that difficulty had set in motion the chain of events that had ultimately led him to La'nah.

But in this instance, Yossi did not "keep his head." Rage consumed him, and not only at his present circumstance. Like so many of us, Yossi was reacting to the *past* in the *present*, to the "attacks and burnings and mobs and running." There was no thought given here to imagining himself, "under the right circumstances, committing" these acts. There was only rage, wild, uncontrollable rage. And forget about pacifism! Yossi wanted to "tear them apart."

As he lay there dying, the face of one of his attackers hovered over him. I recognized it immediately as that of one of my closest and most long-term friends in this life, one who had been nothing but kind and loyal, even when my divorce seemed to divide people into camps about me.

This brought me back to my present life, as Wayne-Daniel. One of the cornerstones of past-life regression is the idea that, out of the myriad lives and incidents we might remember, we are led to the past-life memories best suited to speak to our present life.

What was the violent, angry death of Yossi in the 2nd century saying to me in the 21st?

WAYNE-DANIEL BERARD

Alexander Pope, the great 18th-century poet, wrote in his *Essay on Man* that each individual has what he called a "Ruling Passion."

The ruling passion, be it what it will. The Ruling passion conquers reason still.

Looking back the fourteen years since these regressions, honesty forces me to say that, despite strong tendencies toward kindness and compassion, my Ruling Passion then was anger.

I truly was Yossi's reincarnation. The extent of the isolation, violence, and "othering" in my life had left me with a reservoir of anger that seemed in direct contradiction to the caring, open-hearted, and giving friend, partner, teacher, and Peace Chaplain that also was me. When set upon in ways reminiscent of my soul-rending past, I, too, could explode in ways that left people wondering where *their* Wayne-Daniel had gone.

I was not only disappointed in Yossi. I had been disappointed in myself, my present self, as well.

A case in point: The first Christmas of my separation (leading to divorce) was among the loneliest times of my life. It was winter break from my school, a month that for most was a welcome vacation, but that for me meant only further isolation. I was living

THE LAST ESSENE

alone in a big old house that belonged to friend; it was his family's homestead and, hating to leave it unoccupied, he generously offered it to me for just the cost of utilities. Family dynamics (or their opposite) were making it increasingly difficult for my children to visit me. I did have several close friends who would come by, but my community at my college was an hour's drive away. I heard very little from them. "That's okay," I remember saying to myself, "after the actual Holidays pass, I'm sure they'll come through."

I was very mistaken. The entire month went by, and I heard nary a word from any of them. Could I have reached out? Of course. But after a while, the experience turned into an experiment for me. Who were these people, truly, in my life?

By the first day of spring semester, it appeared that I had my answer.

Upon returning to school, we always asked each other the same question: How was your break? When I encountered the people with whom I thought I was close at my college, I answered that question. In spades!

These were often people who had brought me their life in a basket, asking me to help repair it, people of intense pain and hopelessness. I was glad to be there for them, to spend countless hours in conversation in person and on the phone, to drive to wherever they were. And I was not reluctant to initiate; if I knew one of them was having a difficult time, I would check in with them. I was never too busy.

During those first few days of the new term, I let my anger loose! I "tore these 'friends' apart,"—verbally, of course. I spared no vitriol. Then I turned and walked away.

Several of them approached me in the proceeding weeks to ask for forgiveness and another chance. I was glad to give this. Others left the circle of my life permanently.

Later, in therapy with Eve about my "Ruling Passion," we examined this incident among others. I had to admit to not being proud of myself. I had not sat down and talked about my hurt with these friends, forthrightly and without gloss. I had attacked. I was good with the weapon that words can be. I wanted to hurt them.

Eve helped me to see that I was reacting largely to my past in the present; that those less-than-optimal friends actually represented *all* those who had made my life so miserable for so long.

Then we spoke about expectations.

What Eve next shared with me was very difficult for me to hear, but not in the way one might think.

THE LAST ESSENE

"Wayne-Daniel," she said to me, "you have a greater capacity for caring than almost anyone I have ever known. But you make a very common mistake: You assume that everyone is like you."

My insides shuddered at what she was saying (and even now they twinge as I write this). I had been raised in a tradition in which personal virtues or strengths were never commented on—that way led the path of pride and conceit. If you did or were something good, well, you were supposed to; you got no credit for that. Your faults and failings, however, would be magnified to the nth degree. The model was the Publican from Jesus' parable, the man who would only remain in the back of the house of prayer, beating his breast and repeating, "Lord, have mercy on me, a sinner." (To this day, the front pews in Catholic churches often remain empty, it being considered self-aggrandizing to sit there).

Yes, it was far more difficult for me to hear Eve describe me as having a great capacity for caring than to listen to her ideas about my assumptions regarding others. And those assumptions were just as tied to my childhood spirituality as Yossi's were to his.

To "assume that everyone was like me" was to guarantee that I never broke that unwritten but overriding commandment, "Thou shalt not go thinking you're something." And I was beginning to see that this also involved a very un-Shekinahesque view not only of myself but of the Divine.

I remember well Rabbi Alan (Reb Ishmael in my past life) commenting on something worthwhile I had done or accomplished. "Yes, thanks be to God," I'd replied.

"Will you *stop* saying that!" Alan said to me, visibly upset.

"What? You're a rabbi!" I replied stunned. "You want me to stop thanking God?"

"I want you start thanking you, as well!" Alan replied. "You compulsively say those words, anytime you're complimented on anything. Why do you think that is?"

It took me a while to figure out that the answer was fear. The concept of God that I'd inherited and apparently still partially believed in was one of jealousy and tribute. If I didn't give God *all* the credit for my gifts and abilities, the little boy in me was afraid he would *take them away*.

This was not the Feminine God—nor the Masculine, for that matter. This was Moloch, the demon God-concept, the one to whom some ancient people would sacrifice other human beings, including their own children, to avoid incurring displeasure.

"Wayne-Daniel," Eve went in to say, and in her words I heard (again) the voice of the Shekinah, "Some people have oceans inside them; some people have shot glasses! But when they are full, both the ocean and the shot glass are as full as they can be."

I felt her point deeply. I could not expect others to be more than who they were, and it was not an affront to me if that were the case. Neither was it an affront to God for me to be who I was.

Did I truly have to actively worry that pride and conceit would follow from this? Eve thought it unlikely, and with her help that reservoir of anger within me shrank to a circumnavigable pond; I could consciously walk around it, return to the starting point, and allow its mud to settle and its waters to clear.

Plus, I doubt very much that my Lovely Christine would ever let conceit and pride happen for me!

Was I still disappointed in Yossi?

No.

Regression had taught me that each life I had lived prepared me for the next, and that each fit into the universal mosaic of lives that was my Process of Becoming. I had been intimately familiar with the saying, "Jesus died for our sins." Now I was learning the great truth that Yossi had died, and lived, for my *blessing*, as had every incarnation I had ever experienced, as was the one I was living right now.

Such was the great teaching that the death of Yossi, the once Essene and future seminarian, had imparted to me. I could not be further from disappointed.

Besides, as I was about to experience, the learning was far from over.

CHAPTER 21

Impossible Heart

Past Life Regression

Session 12

Before we began, Sylvia went over some possible elements of this stage of the work. She explained that the Higher Self would continue to direct the experience in the ways that would most benefit my present life. She said that there were often "presences," "Masters," that helped to clarify questions one might have about the past life and its relationship to the present one. These Masters might be experienced as physical forms or in feelings. (I had read about this in Dr. Weiss' books). I asked if she did more facilitating or guiding in this stage, and she replied that she often did. We had a very informative discussion of all this, and then Sylvia asked if I was ready to begin.

After first checking with the Higher Self and the Subconscious (as we always do), Sylvia led me into the meditation. She explained that I might find myself back in the last moments of the past life or in that "in-between" state when the spirit has left the body. It didn't seem to *take long to get to that state. I felt that same feeling of great ease, of softness, of being "inside" everything. Sylvia asked if the spirit had left the body, and I replied that it had. But, unlike the last time, I did see something in this state. It was an eye; it was clearly a woman's eye, almond-shaped with a slight tilt to it. It was the left eye, as it was on the right side of my field of vision. The eye was clearly focused on me, very tender in its expression. It didn't look like some eye floating in space; rather, it was more the impression of an eye, like one gets from one of those with which you emboss a piece of paper. Very soft and part of the atmosphere of the place.*

Then the eye was gone. I described to Sylvia the peace and softness of the place, and how restful it was. She replied that I could stay there and rest as long as I needed, and to let her know when I was ready for anything else. After a few seconds, I did say that I felt like I could ask and listen, although I certainly wasn't ready to leave this state and go into another life.

Sylvia asked if there was anything unreconciled or left up in the air from the past life that I would like to know about now. I said that I was aware that Yaakov (Abba) had left the compound after my death, he and Cush together. That Cush had built them a sort of hut on that place by the river, and the two of them lived there. People would come to see Jacob, to talk about their lives. He would sit, back to back, on the ground with them and listen. Then he would have them go into the river and dip three times. This is how he lived out the rest of his life, in peace.

THE LAST ESSENE

Cush, however, became very bitter and despondent when Jacob finally died. He'd lost everyone. (I could feel these things from him). He started to walk home to Egypt, became a bandit and a murderer. When he finally got back to Alexandria, he threw himself down before the ark in the Christoi synagogue and begged for forgiveness. Then he went into the desert to join "the old men." (These were precursors of the "Desert Fathers," Christian hermits and monks). He lived with them the rest of his life and did find peace there.

Sylvia then asked me if there were any presences in this state with me. I answered that this was a womb, a place to be held and to be born from. At that point, I became aware that I was being "held," as if lying down with my head on someone's arm. At least that was what the feeling would correspond to if it were physical. It was a feeling of immense, tender love. The place was all love. Sylvia asked who this someone was, and I replied that it was the Mother, the Great Mother. I could experience her face looking down at me, with those same eyes I had seen earlier. I said, "This is her womb. This is the womb of the Mother." I also sensed other presences, sort of huddled around us, but not as distinctive as she.

Sylvia asked if she was saying anything. It was funny; I felt the feelings corresponding to words and ideas, but without the actual hearing. It was as if that process was by-passed and we went right to the inner reactions that hearing words would produce. So, although I would sometimes use the verb "to say" when relating this to Sylvia, it was more like "being aware" that this or that was being communicated.

(I have trouble remembering all of this word for word. I'm glad that Sylvia took notes).

I was aware of The Mother saying, "You're here, Shalach. You're well?"

I answered, "Yes, I'm well. Thank you, Ema."

She then said, "So, which did you find better, Shalach? Navee meelot or navee lev, navee chayah?" (I'm writing these more or less phonetically. The only words I recognized were "shalach," which means "sent," and "navee," which, from studying with Alan, I know means "prophet." I only know the term "lev" from the title My Name I Asher Lev, *which I'd never read).*

I felt myself hesitating. "I thought navee lev would be better. But people didn't listen. But it (navee lev) was hard, too. Very hard."

I'm having real difficulty remembering the exact conversation, but I do recall the content. The Mother reminded me that I had chosen the life I'd experienced, to be "navee lev." I had chosen to go to people who didn't have children, who were "empty" and "hurting so badly." She brought up Avel, who had no children; Amma, who (it turns out) could not have children and so cared for others' children. This was why she was afraid to engage in any real affection with them, because she knew they would be going. I (Yossi) was the first one to have held her, to have reached out to her first. "Someone has to be first," I said. And even though she knew I had to go, it apparently made a difference. She began to show affection for Dothan and Ruth. It even made a difference to Dothan that I had held him rather than hurt him. Pote, likewise, had no children, had been afraid to take a wife and have a family because of his "secret faith" and what might happen to him and a family if he were found out. But I was a son to him. The same for "Abba" Jacob, who needed another chance with a son so badly.

So, I had actually chosen that life, to be "sent" in that way. "Sometimes the heart is what's needed," she said, "not words."

I did ask, "Does it always have to be old wells?" And she said that old wells were the past, that people threw things there when they threatened that past way. She also said that sometimes people hide in an old well, in the past, or try to recreate it. I then realized that I (Yossi) had felt guilty about fleeing the Essene compound, that I would sometimes think that I should have stayed hidden there in the wall, behind the grate. That maybe afterward I could have helped. I hid in the well, hoping I could help La'nah as soon as things were quiet, but I had only saved myself. That was part of the reason I'd wanted to throw myself back in the well, out of guilt. But the mother said, "You can't always help everyone, Shalach."

I asked, "Where were you, Ema?" She said, "I was what held you up." I then knew that the feelings I felt in this womb had always been with me, buoying me. She spoke again about heart. She said that people thought it was not possible to really love, especially with so much hurt. "You are the impossible heart," she said. "You showed me to them, reminded them of this place. Thank you, Shalach. I know it was hard for you. You did well."

I said, "But I turned and attacked those people throwing the rocks at me? I gave up on everything I'd been doing." She said, "You don't have to be perfect, Shalach." She asked me to remember Abba and the others I'd been with. "You'd done enough," she said. "It was time for rest."

Then she said a phrase that she'd repeat several times: "Shalach, Aliyah, Shabbat. Then again, Shalach." "Sent, Return, Sabbath. Then again, Sent."

I said that I'd had such a short time with "All My Love." She said, "Business trip. You go off for a while, but you come back home to her. Then you go again." The Mother said that "she has already gone on to her next place. She'll wait for you there." The mother would remind me that I had seen all this and had chosen it. She said, "But you don't have to be Shalach. You don't have to be anything. You can stay here, if you choose. You don't have to go on."

But I said that, yes, I'd like to go on. After shabbat. That, after all, "All My Love" had gone on. That I would stay Shalach.

Things got quiet. Sylvia asked me if there was anything more from this experience. I signaled "No." And she led me out of the regression.

THE LAST ESSENE

When I got home, I looked up the words "lev" and "meelot." "Meelot" means "words," and "lev" means "heart." "Navee meelot"—prophet of words, of talking? "Navee lev, navee chaya"—prophet of the heart, prophet of living?

The three of us did talk together a little about the regression. Sylvia made it clear that if there was more I needed to process, we could have more sessions. We all thought it interesting that I hadn't asked about my (Yossi's) birth parents. It had never entered my mind. We thought that perhaps, as I had chosen that life, to not live with birth parents and to be, in essence, a child for those who had none, it just might not be important who Yossi's birth parents were?

In this, what may be my final session with Sylvia, I was led again to what, for lack of a better name, is often called "The In-Between State," the state between incarnations.

I had been very pleasantly, I would say soothingly, surprised by my memory of Yossi's death experience. *I didn't feel like I went anywhere, but rather everything else fell away. I did have a distinct sense of being "inside" of things, or rather, that I always had been, but now the "outside" had dissolved, like it was just an idea or a thought.*

What an amazing realization! The "essential me" had always been on the "inside of things"; this physical reality was more like an idea or a thought than anything else. In death, I did not go anywhere; *it* did!

And there was that beautiful, feminine eye that I had caught a glimpse of in previous sessions. This, I now knew, was the Divine Feminine, always keeping me in mind and in sight. Now I was experiencing her as the Great Mother (*Rachamim* in Hebrew)—how comforting *and* empowering for an orphan across lifetimes to know this protection and love!

The "felt words" of my conversation with the Great Mother seemed to defy the ability of words themselves to convey experience. Inadequate as this "translation" might be, the sense of it was overwhelmingly manifest to me.

First, She called me by my truest name, my Hebrew name, *Shalach*. I had discovered this name in what I can only describe as a mystical experience. Decades before, still in grad school, I had been lying on my bed writing in my journal. Suddenly, I "heard" a sound, although not really with my ears. Looking back, this was very much the same phenomenon I would describe to Sylvia in this session: *I felt the feelings corresponding to words and ideas, but without the actual hearing. It was as if that process was by-passed and we went right to the inner reactions that hearing words would produce.* Only, on this occasion, this word was accompanied by a very physical, but yet otherworldly, sensation; as the word spoke itself, it felt as if a door in the very fabric of reality itself opened and closed. The word was "Shalach," and that metaphysical doorway opened and closed itself with each syllable: *"Sha"—open, "lach"—close.*

I remember jumping up in bed! What the hell was this? Was I losing my mind? I waited, listened. Nothing happened. I returned to my journal writing. Then, suddenly it manifested itself again: *"Sha"—open, "lach"—close.* An unmistakable sense of being called was essential to this. In some sense, this word was my name, was who I truly was.

At the time, I had not even begun to search for my birth families; I had never even considered the idea that I could be Jewish. I was in a class on Scotts Literature that term, which included works in Scotts Gaelic. To me, the aspirated sound of the "ch" in Shalach sounded very much like this language. I went to the Gaelic dictionary I'd purchased for the course. "Shalach" meant "dirtied" or "soiled."

Well, *"nach raibh sé sin go hálainn?!"* ("Wasn't that lovely?!" Gaelic).

Fast-forward decades. I had found my birth families, embraced my Jewishness, and was in Torah study with Rabbi Alan. As he went over some of the glowingly Hebrew words of the passage we were studying, I recalled that mystical event. After the study, I asked him if he had ever heard of the word, "Shalach."

"Of course," he said. "It's Hebrew for 'Sent.' Someone who has been sent is called 'Shalach.'"

Apparently, here in the In-Between State, the Great Mother was referring to me as one who had been "Sent." Sent for what?

It would seem I'd had a mission, as Yossi—one involving learning.

"So, which did you find better, Shalach? *Navee meelot or navee lev, navee chayah?*"

The word "navee" in Hebrew means "prophet." Again, that ingrained inhibition against "thinking you're something" reared its head. Yossi, a prophet? But he had delivered no inspired messages to kings or nations?

And such, apparently, had been exactly the point.

In terms of my incarnation as Yossi, the Great Mother was asking which I had found better, to be a *navee meelot* or a *navee lev, a navee chaya*. In that In-Between State, I answered without consciously knowing the meaning of all those words. Once I looked them up, I discovered they meant "prophet of words" and "prophet of the heart, prophet of living," respectively.

If I had not been in this incredibly peaceful, shock-proof "place," I would have been blown away! It would seem that at least one of the purposes of my incarnation as Yossi was to discover which form of "speaking for God' was "better"—words or the heart? Perhaps in a previous life I had been a *"navee meelot,"* perhaps I had attempted to use words to communicate Godness to those to whom I had been "sent." Apparently, that experience had been quite difficult; a traditional prophet's audience was famously unreceptive.

> *"I thought navee lev would be better. But people didn't listen. But it (navee lev) was hard, too. Very hard."*

And how did one be a *navee lev*, a heart prophet? Not, apparently, with words, but with love itself—choosing love over the demands of its restrictive opposite, no matter what robes of holiness it wore. Sitting with those in pain, accompanying, not fixing. Accepting the same from others, too. Helping to relieve the burdens of the guilt-ridden and the repentant, forgiving even the most devastating acts, to the best of your always-human abilities.

Yes, being *navee lev* was hard, very hard. Yossi's life and that of those who had loved and supported him bore testimony to that. It was one thing for one's words not to be heard, one's truth to be disastrously, often fatally ignored. But to lose one's beloveds—wives, husbands, children, friends, parents (birth and found), teachers, communities—over and over again? If only

love is real, then only love's loss is real pain.

WAYNE-DANIEL BERARD

And how does the prophet of the heart respond? What is their prophecy?

To love anyway. To forgive anyway. For,

though dull were all we taste as bright,

bitter utterly all things sweet . . .

and nothing quite as least as truth

—I say though hate were why men breathe—

. . . love is the whole and more than all

—ee cummings

Such, the life I had been had taught me, was how a *navee lev* met the polarization, the yearning for mere incivility in the face of murderous otherness, the existential exhaustion of insistence on acceptance. To love anyway. To forgive anyway. Including, and most especially, one's self.

There in the In-Between State, I had reinforced what I had read in Dr. Weiss' books, that we choose the reincarnation into which we enter. I had specifically chosen to enter the lives of those who had no birth-children or no longer had them, from Avel to Amma, from Pote to Jacob—and yes, in my present life, my adoptive parents, as well. This was another way in which the heart could engage prophecy, by fulfilling the age-old promises, across scriptures and traditions, of relief for the childless.

But what, after all, was the answer to the question I was being asked? Which *was* better, *navee meelot* or *navee lev?* To be a prophet of words or of love?

The answer, I had come to find, was "Yes."

Yossi and I had both learned that the Process of Becoming was not a way of exclusion. The words and the heart were not mutually exclusive, and when we fall into the trap of thinking them so, this is when hatred and violence begin to hold sway. We can become so committed to our words, sacred and secular, that no amount of harm they might do touches our hearts. And we can likewise be so enshrined, so invested in all the heart has experienced, especially its pain, that no amount or form of words can touch it. "We know so much about how hatred works," Elie Wiesel has said. "We know it starts with words, with symbols, and it ends with killing." Yossi knew this, too; he had experienced first-hand an era of history in which words and symbols which sought to represent God had devolved into hatred and killing. And the inverse of Professor Wiesel's statement was likewise true: Violence and killing can deaden the heart of even those most committed to words and symbols of Love.

It was a very hard lesson, so hard that it took more than one lifetime to even begin to learn, but there was no difference between word and heart. To truly say it was to be it (is this not how the God of Genesis created?), and to be it without saying it was not to truly be at all. Hadn't Rabbi Alan informed we students that the word for "word" in Hebrew and the word for "thing" are one and the same?

There was no contradiction between Yossi's work as scholar of words and his sitting in silence with those who suffered. They were one and the same. Yossi had been a witness, in word and heart, to the Divine Inclusion in a world careening toward walls that became barricades, and barricades only invite storming. He had suffered for this, but he had been true.

And what of his reincarnation, eighteen centuries later? Had I, as Wayne-Daniel—orphan, adoptee, spiritual seeker, teacher, writer, ex-Catholic seminarian, present-day Renewal Jew, Peace Chaplain, beloved of the Lovely Christine—had all my lives finally shown me that the answer was always "Yes, and"? Could I "un-mutually exclude" words (the Head) and love (the Heart)?

Not long ago, I posted this original poem online:

Exception

When the darkest possible

THE LAST ESSENE

darkness wells from

the ground up, and

you say, "I am only

alone," think

and say, "Except

for him." When you

feel completely

unlovable, stop

and know I am

your ever exception.

If you fear "My

fundamental

wrongness

dooms me,"

look again;

there I am

walking up

your garden path.

When you are sinking

down and down into

"nobody cares and

WAYNE-DANIEL BERARD

I don't blame them,"

reach down that

much further, find

that slip with

my number in

the depths of

your pocket or

purse, yes, call

it, call me "2:30

AM," you say,

"I can't possibly.

He can't mean

it." You can, he

does. I will

never abandon

you, not even

to you. I am

that exception,

I am that friend.

The response was heart-warming and word-affirming. Words had come home to the heart, and a poem had shown that the word for "Love" and Love itself could be the same.

Perhaps this little book could do that also?

It wasn't exactly writing Talmud (been there, done that). But it was true.

Ema, The Great Mother, called both Yossi and my present self the "Impossible Heart." She said that I (the "me" across incarnations; in the In-Between the lines blurred) had shown people that it was still possible to love, even with so much hurt. Her affirmation was the whole and more than all.

She also repeated three words to me: *"Shalach, Aliyah, Shabbat. Then again, Shalach."* These mean "Sent, Return, Rest," then "Sent" again. This was the way of reincarnation and of the In-Between State: first, we are sent out into a life, eventually we return to this state from which we came; then we rest, and then can be sent out again in a new incarnation.

If and when we want to.

It seemed important to Ema that I understand this: No one *has* to be reincarnated. They can remain in the In-Between State "indefinitely." (Would this, then, be their "heaven"?)

When I asked about my "All My Love," the soul who had been La'nah in my past-life and was Christine in this one, The Great Mother used the interesting term "Business Trip—we each go off into the business of Becoming but are reunited again in various lives and in the In-Between. At that "moment," La'nah/Christine had "gone on to her next place." Ema reassured me that All My Love would meet me there, once again.

This leads to some very interesting points about past-life and present-life.

There, in Sylvia's office, I was remembering Yossi's experience of the In-Between State, after his death in the 2nd century CE. In that experience, he had been told that his Great Love had already gone on to her next incarnation, where she awaited him. Was this the life which Christine and I now lived together? Was that even possible, with so much time intervening?

One of the results of my work with Sylvia was a strong desire to add past-life regression to the quiver of services I could offer to others as a Peace Chaplain and as the chaplain of my college. I

THE LAST ESSENE

sought out the training sessions that Dr. Weiss offers and attended one at the Omega Institute in Rhinebeck, NY, a place of incredible energy-insight the likes of which I had never known. There I experienced several regressions, including memories of the In-Between State. I recall them quite clearly.

In that state, I could see arrayed before me, as in a rows in a stadium, all the lives I had already lived, as well as all those I would yet live. And even more importantly, I could see how they all intersected, interconnected, how each led from and to the other in the School of Becoming which was human reality. I could understand how someone, from this vantage point, could choose a life of hardship and pain, because they saw and understood that life's essential role in their becoming a thoroughly compassionate, fully realized human being. I came to a much deeper understanding of karma than merely "what goes around comes around"; karma existed for the sake of learning and growth, not reward and punishment.

As for time itself, it became clear to me that it was largely irrelevant to this process. We truly were, as the great theologian and scientist Teilhard de Chardin had said, "Spiritual beings having a human experience." As such, our essential being extends beyond time *and* through it—imagine yourself lying on the floor at a doorway connecting several rooms. Your head might be in one room, your torso in another, your midsection in another, and your legs and feet in yet another. In the same way, the spiritual beings that we are extend from the In-Between State, which is outside of time and space, through any number of incarnations— lives each as different as differing rooms, but all still essentially us, and all basically happening at the same "time." This means that my life as Yossi, my life as Wayne-Daniel, and any number of other lives are all running simultaneously, like parallel streams of energy, only one of which we are aware of at one time . . . mostly! Have we ever experienced premonitions, memories, flashes of realities we can't explain? Perhaps now we can.

From this vantage point, we can see that it is possible for us to choose a next incarnation in 2020, and the one "after" that in 1320. It makes no difference! La'nah/Christine could next await me in any time, any place.

"Time present and time past / Are both perhaps present in time future, / And time future contained in time past," proclaims the poet on whom I wrote a doctoral dissertation, T. S. Eliot.

"All is love. With love comes understanding. With understanding comes patience. And then time stops. And everything is now," explains the Master Healer who taught me and so many others the truth of our lives, Brian Weiss.

Isn't *that* lovely?

CHAPTER 22

All Mothers, Great and Small

Session 13

Sylvia and I (and Christine) did have one more "wrap up" session several weeks later. In that interim, I experienced what seemed to be rather spontaneous regressions, always during my daily meditation. I was not trying to have these experiences; they just happened on their own. In some, I would just see flashes of scenes I'd already described to Sylvia. Others would be new: I would see Ruth playing alone, wishing I would return as I said I would. I would see scenes of Alexandria and note how primitive life was then. Often, I would be in the Egyptian quarter with Pote, looking at a wall of a building that served as a sort of graffiti bulletin board. I would ask Pote the significance of this or that sign or phrase.

However, I did have a very detailed and rather complete spontaneous regression during one meditation session. Very plainly, I saw a young woman, half-lying, half-sitting in the dusty ground. Around her was chaos, as her village was being destroyed by soldiers. Her back was to me; she wore a faded, dark reddish head scarf that ran down her back. Then a soldier rode by her on a horse. He worked for the Romans but was not Roman himself; he was much darker and wore a helmet with a curlicue crest. He had a bow slung across his back and a leather quiver of arrows on his saddle. He passed the girl, then whirled around and came back. I knew he was going to rape her.

The scene shifted. I saw this same young woman, a very young face, very pretty, dark, heavily lidded eyes. She was walking along a dirt path in a desert region, rather disoriented. If you looked closely, you could see she was just showing a pregnancy. She had come into the area to get away from people, to save herself and her unborn child, as the penalty for being pregnant and unwed, regardless of the circumstances, was quite severe.

Next, I saw her in a cave, just past its mouth. She is extremely tired, as the cave is high up a barren hill, one of many there. This is where she is living (it is one of the same series of caves my friend, Fred, would one day keep me from reaching in my 20th-century trip to Qumran). She walks out from the cave; down below I can see a compound; it is the same one I will live in. The sun is setting behind it and to the left. She is walking very carefully and stealthily down the slope. She approaches an area a bit beyond the wall; it smells and feels funny. This is the garbage dump for the compound; she begins rifling around, looking for food or any scrap of anything she can use. This is how she has been sustaining herself. The Essenes don't come out after sunset, so she feels fairly safe.

THE LAST ESSENE

Suddenly, she hears a rustle. A man is coming, an Essene with a big copper trough. He is late dumping the garbage. He sees here; he shouts out to her. She begins to run, but he drops the trough and follows her. He is faster; she drops to her face, grabs his feet, and begs him for mercy. He backs away; he doesn't like her touch. He asks what she is doing there. She begins to tell him; he tells her to stand, and he sees she is very pregnant. He asks where she has been living, and she points toward the hills. "Show me," he says.

The man is Avel, although he looks much younger. She leads him up to her cave. He looks around, it is now almost dark but there is a nearly full moon. He says that it would be a sin for him to allow anything to happen to the child, so he will help her with food, etc. But she must stay up here and never go down toward the compound. If she is caught, she must swear to say that all she had in the cave she had collected at the dump. She agrees. She wonders what he will want in return, but she doesn't say anything about it, and neither does he.

He comes almost every day at differing times. He brings her skins of water, food, old blankets, a broken stool (she sets one end on a rock). Slowly they begin to speak to each other. He doesn't know her name and doesn't ask her; in his head he calls her "Chavah" (Hebrew for "Eve"), as she is the first woman in his life. She tells him of her attack; he tells her how he had run away from home after botching his bar mitzvah, the failed son of a brilliant father. He had come to the Essenes, who had taken him in. He is in charge of all the orphans the group raises; it is their practice. She talks about giving him her child, if it is a boy, to take to the compound, saying it had been abandoned in the dump. He agrees to this, only inside he has a great, gut-wrenching struggle. He has feelings for this woman; part of him wants to tell her so, to offer to marry her, to leave the Essenes and raise her child with her. He is terribly torn.

One night at sunset, he comes to the cave and finds Chavah dead. She has died in childbirth. A baby boy is lying on her stomach, the umbilical cord still attached. Avel is beside himself. The child is not crying at all. Avel takes the child and cuts the cord. He then places it on the blanket next to his mother. Avel takes a copper pot that he had once brought and begins to dig with it next to the woman. He buries her there, takes the boy back to the compound, and says that he found him in the dump. He had searched the area, he says, but could find no one else. The boy joins the ranks of the other orphans with the Essenes. With the Righteous One's consent, (the Essene leader) Avel names him Yosiah—Yossi—which means, "God is fire." Avel remembers the fire he felt within himself for Chavah.

Addendum: Much later, I recognized this woman, my mother, as Samantha, a woman I met in an Alan Study. She mentioned in class that she was looking for work; my department at school was looking for adjunct faculty. I made the introductions and Sam came to my college. We became friends (never too late to be friends with your mom!) On that first day, after showing her where the copy machines were and introducing her to everyone we crossed paths with, we sat over coffee. I said to her, "How do you feel about reincarnation?" and proceeded to explain that she had been my mother in a past life. I thanked her profusely for having had me, for all she had suffered to keep me safe before my birth. She took the news very well! (As a matter of fact, in subsequently discussions, if we ever saw things differently, she would laugh and say, "Now, don't argue with your mother!)

THE LAST ESSENE

Commentary from Sylvia

I have no sense of how long it took to integrate the regression as fully as W-D notes in these writings. I do know that his integration is as complete and far reaching as any I have known from one lifetime's lessons. Kudos for that. It is a remarkable achievement.

Wayne-Daniel ends his story with the idea of 'learning'. There is a movement to the word, a sense of ongoing forward momentum through time. To me, this is one of the pillars of life's purpose—to learn and to grow. It is akin to the concept of hope.

Wayne-Daniel has shown us a beautiful example of a certain kind of learning about one's soul's trajectory, having gone into the depths and details of one past-life story and relating the learning to one's current life.

He chose, through intuition, a pivotal life, one where much can be explained about the lives that followed it up until the present. Doing this has illuminated and freed him from the constraints posed by the traumas of that life.

When you grow you leave something behind—maybe not as dramatic as the cocoon of the butterfly but something akin: old structures, now left behind, allowing one to move into a new reality freed of those constrictions. Wayne-Daniel in this effort has had a true unburdening, release and opening for growth.

Because the personal traumas of this life story take place within a context of religious factionalism and violence there is an obvious resonance to those same forces that continue to play out in current world affairs, in tribalism of all kinds. Tuning into the past life dimension helps explain humankind's entrenched tribal attachments, along with the legacies we also hold through our ancestral ties. This can feel daunting: how will humans ever be free of the past?

But there is also hope offered in Wayne-Daniel's endeavor. In his effort we see that humans at some core level long to be free.

I personally believe that there is a force inside and larger than ourselves that pulls for individual growth and group, even species, evolution. Further, it is life affirming to notice and celebrate that impulse inside ourselves, and to note the myriad examples of people aligning with this creative energy. It often involves hard work that at some point becomes exhilarating. Wayne-Daniel has shown such an example in his connecting and integrating the Yossi part of himself.

This can be an inspiration for us all who are lucky enough to be able to harness the right will, commitment, and open heartedness.

POSTLUDE

The Well

A traveler came to a well . . . just in time, for he was nearly dead from thirst, and this was the only well for untold miles.

As he came nearer, however, he saw a number of people lying about—near, around, even draped across the lip of the well. Puzzlement soon turned to horror; all were dead.

Cautiously, the traveler approached, and things began to clarify themselves. He found no rope, no bucket, no winch or handle—no way to draw water from the well. The traveler peered over the stone rim; he could neither see nor sense a bottom. The others had clearly all thirsted to death.

The traveler sat and began to ponder. These others could not have died immediately. He saw that one still held fast to the ankle of another, and that one to another's. And that last body, leaning, even in death's paralysis, down into the well—he must have been the final link in a desperate human chain. The traveler supposed that each one had planned to take his or her turn at the end of the chain. The set of the last man's arms, grasping emptily into space, made the traveler's soul shudder. Was death by drowning better than death by thirst? Quicker, at least?

As he stood, hunched over the useless well, the traveler heard a distant sound, like a humming. As it grew closer, he could tell that it was a chant, a *niggun,* a song without words. But somehow each tone was a word-seed that shot to full flower inside him the moment he heard it.

Barukhu,

Dear One,

Shekinah,

Holy Name,

    When I call on

        the light of my soul,

I come home . . .*

The chanter came on, a tall burly man. Jewish, the traveler thought. Beard. Shirt in lumberjack plaid. Saul Bunyan.

"No rope. No bucket," the traveler said. "No water."

"Just call to it," said the other. "Just say what you want. Out loud."

"Delirium," the traveler thought to himself. *"Thirst will do that."*

But what he said was, "I'm afraid there are the dead down there."

The big man just shrugged, like clouds separating from mountains.

"Just call."

Why would one retain the fear of being murdered by a madman, even when facing certain death from thirst? Nonetheless.

The traveler leaned over the mouth of the well and called out, "Water, rise up! I need a drink!"

He turned to the stranger. Then back again. He'd picked up the faint, soundless sound of water muffling the echo of stones in a round, narrow space. Then, the noise shifted; the traveler, who'd once spent a day and night listening to the quick trills of water peaking across a sheltered cove, recognized it. He dipped a finger below the well's perimeter—water, up to his second knuckle! He cupped his hands and drank.

"If only the others had known," he said, between cool, clear draughts.

"I told them," said the stranger.

The traveler arched an eyebrow.

"Look again," the other answered.

The traveler went from body to body. Each had his face.

He backed away, aghast, bumped into the well, and felt a cold, clammy touch against his shoulders. He cried out and leapt aside; the blank, waterlogged face bobbing at him likewise was his own. He put his hands over his eyes. *"Dear One! Dear One!"* he shouted.

When he lowered them again, the scene was very still. The bodies were gone; the stranger had likewise disappeared. The well was as it had been, water receded into its depths.

"What? Here again?" the traveler thought. *"Oh no."*

THE LAST ESSENE

Then he noticed a figure in the hot, humming distance. A woman.

She came closer and closer.

Her hair . . . it was a light-filled dark; he struggled to find the words (*fiber-optic? night's brimming dawness inspiring artifact? if he could run his hands through it, of what would he ever need be informed?*)

And her eyes were blue, that child's blue when the sun and the moon are there at the same time. Two holes in the sky. He'd asked his parents, *"Where do the cut-out circles go?"* Now he knew.

"Who are you?" he wanted to ask.

"You called me," she said.

* Lyrics, Rabbi Lev Friedman

ABOUT THE AUTHOR

Wayne-Daniel Berard, PhD, is an educator, poet, writer, shaman, sage, and Gryffindor. Wayne-Daniel lives in Mansfield, MA with his wife, The Lovely Christine.

ABOUT THE PRESS

Unsolicited Press is based out of Portland, Oregon and focuses on the works of the unsung and underrepresented. As a womxn-owned, all-volunteer small publisher that doesn't worry about profits as much as championing exceptional literature, we have the privilege of partnering with authors skirting the fringes of the lit world. We've worked with emerging and award-winning authors such as Shann Ray, Amy Shimshon-Santo, Brook Bhagat, Kris Amos, and John W. Bateman.

Learn more at unsolicitedpress.com. Find us on X (formerly Twitter) and Instagram.

Milton Keynes UK
Ingram Content Group UK Ltd.
UKHW031947281024
450365UK00008B/483